Praise For *Paris, My Sweet*

"Amy's adventures in *Paris, My Sweet* are of fairy tale magnitude. Her story is infectious and contagious in every way and has reminded me of so many of my own memories walking down those very streets and nibbling on those one-of-a-kind Parisian treats. This book made me smile."

—Johnny Iuzzini, James Beard Award Winner, Author of *Dessert FourPlay*, Head Judge *Top Chef Just Desserts*

"From the New York cupcake wars to the perfect Parisian macaron, Thomas's passion is palpable; her sweet tooth, unstoppable."

—Elizabeth Bard, bestselling author of *Lunch in Paris*

"Follow Amy Thomas's quest in Paris to find the tastiest chocolates, towering *gâteaux*, and most sublime macarons while crisscrossing the Atlantic. Like a tasty Parisian bonbon, this book is filled with sweet surprises."

—David Lebovitz, *New York Times* bestselling author of *The Sweet Life in Paris*

"Dessert lovers will devour this one…Amy Thomas draws the reader into the comfort of sweets seemingly found on every street corner in Paris, creating a delectable fantasy world. As a self-professed sugarholic, this memoir/travelogue/dessert guide to New York and Paris is a rare, nostalgic treat— equal parts charm, style, and wit."

—Pichet Ong, chef and author of *The Sweet Spot*

"More than just a tasty treat, *Paris, My Sweet* is a lot like fine chocolate—deep, rich, and complex."
—Jamie Cat Callan, author of *French Women Don't Sleep Alone* and *Bonjour, Happiness!*

"Amy Thomas seduces us in the same manner that Paris seduced her—one exquisite morsel at a time."
—Nichole Robertson, author of *Paris in Color*

"Such a charming, heartfelt book. *Paris, My Sweet* is as dainty and decadent as a box of pastel macarons, a bewitching tale of a young woman's love affair with two iconic cities and the confections found in each one."
—Ann Mah, author of *Kitchen Chinese*

"Amy Thomas's descriptions of the delicious delights in Paris and New York had me almost licking the pages."
—Rachel Khoo, author of *Little Paris Kitchen*

"A sweet and charming tale of Paris through the eyes of a cake-lover. Willie Wonka for grown ups—and a guide to some of the sweetest destinations in the City of Light."
—Karen Wheeler, author of *Tout Sweet*

Paris,

MY SWEET

A YEAR IN THE CITY OF LIGHT
(AND DARK CHOCOLATE)

—[AMY THOMAS]—

sourcebooks

Published by Sourcebooks, Inc.
P.O. Box 4410, Naperville, Illinois 60567-4410
(630) 961-3900
Fax: (630) 961-2168
www.sourcebooks.com

Library of Congress Cataloging-in-Publication Data
Thomas, Amy
Paris, my sweet : a love letter in madeleines, chocolate, and croissants / Amy Thomas.
    p. cm.
(pbk. : alk. paper) 1. Pastry--France--Paris--Guidebooks. 2. Paris (France)—Guidebooks. I. Title.
 TX773.T494 2012
 641.86'50944361—dc23

2011042786

Printed and bound in the United States of America.
VP 10 9 8 7 6 5 4

To my dear family and friends in the States, who
always supported me and enthused about my life
abroad, but lured me back with their love.

To my new friends in Paris, who kept me sane and
made the experience richer than ever expected.

To everyone who shared my adventure on the blog,
cheering me on, offering support, and writing to me over
the years. Your words meant more than you'll ever know.

To all the brilliant bakers, *pâtissiers*, and *chocolatiers* who took
the time to share their stories and indulge my curiosity.

To Jessica Papin and Shana Drehs, who, through a special
confluence of forces, made sure this book happened.

And to Allyson and Fred, without whom there
would never have been a story to tell.

Merci.

"Nine of every ten persons say they love chocolate. The tenth lies."

—Anthelme Brillat-Savrin

"And I have the firm belief in this now, not only in terms of my own experience but in knowing about the experience of others, that when you follow your bliss, doors will open where you would not have thought there were going to be doors and where there wouldn't be a door for anybody else.

If you follow your bliss, you put yourself on a kind of track, which has been there all the while, waiting for you, and the life that you ought to be living is the one you are living."

—Joseph Campbell

"Your good friend has just taken a piece of cake out of the garbage and eaten it. You will probably need this information when you check me into the Betty Crocker Clinic."

—Miranda to Carrie on *Sex and the City*

AUTHOR'S NOTE

Some names have been changed to protect people's privacy.

CONTENTS

——— ✳ ———

LE TOUR DU CHOCOLAT

I guess you could say my story began with a bicycle and some bonbons. At the time, it just seemed like a fun summer vacation: it was 2008, and I did an apartment swap with someone in Paris. I had already visited earlier that year, but what can I say? When the invitation to spend time in the City of Light (and Dark Chocolate) comes knocking, my first response is "*pourquoi pas?*"

I've just always been one of those girls. I spent a college semester in Paris, and it was then I fell in love with the city's beauty and grace—and Nutella street crepes. When I returned to the States, I wore silk scarves and a black beret; the only thing missing from my clichéd uniform were the Gauloises cigarettes.

I binged on French films, schooling myself in *nouvelle vague* directors, falling especially hard for Eric Rohmer, before contemporary movies like *The City of Lost Children* and *Amélie* seduced me. I studied the Lost Generation, reading Hemingway, Fitzgerald, and Janet Flanner, and built a mini-library so I'd never be far from Paris. I had books about cats in Paris, dogs in Paris, expats in Paris; Parisian interiors, Parisian gardens, and Parisian cuisine, organized by neighborhood; bistros of Paris, *pâtisseries* of Paris, and shopping in Paris. I became a regular at a café in my neighborhood in San Francisco simply because it served *café au lait* in little bowls instead of mugs, and I had more Eiffel Tower tchotchkes than I am comfortable admitting.

I was just another Francophile, like you. Until that summer of 2008.

That trip was the first time I was in Paris during the summer, and it was absolutely amazing. I loved that it was light out until after 10:00 p.m., giving me several extra hours to roam back-alley streets and sit by the Seine. I was excited to discover new neighborhoods like Bercy and Canal Saint-Martin and new "bistronomy" restaurants like Le Verre Volé and Le Comptoir du Relais. I got sucked into the semi-annual sales, *les soldes*, and hooked on Vélib's, the public bike-sharing system.

And then there were all the *chocolatiers*.

By that time, I was just as obsessed with sweets as I was Paris. I had a column in *Metro* newspaper called "Sweet Freak" and a blog by the same name. I knew every bakery, dessert bar, *gelateria*, tea salon, and chocolatier in New York City. When I traveled, I built my itinerary around a town's must-visit sweet spots.

So naturally during that week in Paris, I researched the city's best chocolatiers, mapped out a circuit, and then Vélib'ed between eight of them. It was exhilarating and exhausting, not to mention decadent. It was a chocoholic's dream ride. I wrote about my Tour du Chocolat for the *New York Times*, and it went on to become a top-ten travel story for the year. As I was secretly plotting a way to spend more time eating chocolate in Paris, the in-house recruiter of the ad agency where I worked casually walked into my office one day and asked if I wanted to move to Paris. I was getting transferred to write copy for the iconic fashion label Louis Vuitton. It all happened so suddenly, and seemed so magical, that I had to ask: was Paris my destiny or sheer force of will?

I guess it goes to show that you just never know where life will take you. You search for answers. You wonder what it all means. You stumble, and you soar. And, if you're lucky, you make it to Paris for a while. Here's what happened when I did.

—[CHAPTER 1]—

A WHOLE NEW BATCH OF BONBONS

*C*an one question change your life? I'm willing to bet a twenty-five-piece box of Jean-Paul Hévin bonbons on it.

In the fall of 2008, I was sitting in my office, living what I considered to be a pretty great life. I was single, owned a cute apartment in the East Village, and I was braving New York's dating scene. I had the best friends in the world and a jam-packed social calendar. I enjoyed my job as an advertising copywriter. But what I really loved were my moonlighting dalliances: exploring bakeries, dessert bars, gelaterias, and chocolate boutiques and documenting my delicious discoveries for my "Sweet Freak" blog and *Metro* newspaper column, along with other local magazines and newspapers. You could say my life was good: easy, fun, *comfortable*.

I was enjoying my afternoon bonbon (a piece of 78

percent dark chocolate, hand-delivered by my boss who had brought it back from a business trip to Germany; it had these lovely little bits of cocoa that added a nice semi-crunchy texture to the sharp flavor). I was definitely coasting. My creative directors at Ogilvy & Mather, the agency where I worked, always made sure I wasn't overloaded. Which was a good thing since my best friend, AJ, and I were often in the habit of lingering over kir royales at Keith McNally's fabulous Meatpacking District bistro, Pastis, until 2:00 a.m. On that particular autumn day, I was wondering if Rafaa, the Romanian gazillionaire I had met the night before, was going to call when Allyson, the agency's in-house recruiter, walked into my office.

"What do you think about Paris?" she asked, pausing in the doorway to adjust her Ugg boot. I was surprised to see her. I had been with Ogilvy for two years, so there was rarely a reason for her to come into my office. I put the chocolate aside—already looking forward to getting back to its thin, almost-bitter bite later—and gave her my full attention.

"Why, are you going over for vacation?" I asked, her visit suddenly making sense. A few months prior, I had spent a week in Paris, touring the best chocolatiers on the city's Vélib's—three-speed bicycles stationed all over the city that, for just a euro a day, were there for the taking and leaving. It was genius because it not only allowed me to hit up multiple chocolatiers each day, but also kept my annihilation of the bonbons from going straight to my ass. After my return, three colleagues who were planning trips to Paris had asked me for my must-eat-sweets itinerary. I thought Allyson might be a sweet freak too.

"No," she said, brushing her bangs out of her eyes, still all nonchalant as she took a seat in front of me. "Well, actually, they're looking for an English-speaking writer in the Paris office." Pause. Our eyes locked. "I thought of you." We both started to smile. "On the Louis Vuitton account," she finished dramatically.

I spun myself around in my Aeron chair and laughed. "*What?* They're looking for an English-speaking writer in Paris? To work on Louis Vuitton? And you're asking *me?*" That elicited three nods from Allyson, and suddenly my life was changing.

The next few months were a blur of interviews, portfolio reviews, negotiations, and paperwork. They were also an emotional roller coaster. Of course I wanted to go live in Paris and work with one of the best fashion houses in the world. What Louboutin-loving, Coco-worshipping, macaron addict wouldn't? But what about my cute East Village co-op that my dad, an interior designer, and I had just finished decorating? What about my New York-based freelance network? And my "Sweet Freak" column? What about my circle of friends who, after having graduated from our roaring twenties to our (more or less) refined thirties, were now my modern family?

And my crazy black tabby cat, Milo? What about him? Would I have to leave him behind, or could I get a French work visa *pour deux*?

As I waited forever for an official offer—a little preview of the maddeningly slow pace in Paris—my enthusiasm ebbed and flowed. When I wasn't mentally plotting shopping sprees in the Haut Marais or sunset picnics in the Jardin du Luxembourg, I was hoping the whole thing would fall apart. That way, I wouldn't have to make a decision at all and I could stay in New York, not because I was too chicken to leave, but because circumstances beyond my control kept me there. I read the same ambivalence in my friends' faces. Every time I told a close friend—for, being slightly superstitious, I had been guarding the potential move to Paris from most people in case it fell through—I felt a pang as I watched their face cycle through the emotions: shock, awe, thrill, disbelief, despondence, acceptance, and, finally, enthusiasm.

Although, when I told Rachel Zoe Insler, the chocolatier who had just opened a chocolate boutique in my neighborhood, Bespoke Chocolates, her face immediately shone with envy.

—— ✸ ——

The first time I bit into one of Rachel's truffles, I was instantly smitten. But the first time I met her, I was charmed. She's got the smarts and talent of a chocolatier trained in London, but the cool, down-to-earth vibe of someone who can cop to loving Tasti D-Lite frozen dessert. *How could someone who produces such exquisite specimens of chocolate be so...ordinary?* I wondered. Every time I visited her chocolate shop, tucked in a hidden alley off First Street, she'd be wearing yoga pants and clogs, hair pulled back in a bandana, Jack Johnson playing on iTunes. Shortly after she opened her boutique, we had bonded by sharing our childhood sweets obsessions: hers, Baskin-Robbins bubble gum ice cream, and mine, cream-filled Hostess CupCakes. *So* ordinary.

Rachel had lived in the East Village for years—the only thing that gave her edge. Or so I thought, until I learned about her European training and tasted her amazing chocolates. "Here," she said on one of my early visits, handing me a 70 percent Colombian dark chocolate truffle. "Let's start simple."

It was impossibly creamy, a real melt-in-your-mouth gem. "Good grief, that's amazing, Rachel." She smiled and nodded in agreement. I guess she knew she had a hopeless devotee on her hands. She indulged my insatiability and curiosity by feeding me new flavors on every subsequent visit.

"Oh, that's a good one," I responded to the zingy and aromatic Southampton tea truffle, picking up on hints of apricot in the Ceylon tea. "Heaven," I moaned, gripping the marble countertop where she mixed and tempered her bonbons, after tasting the strawberry balsamic truffle, made with strawberry purée, eight-year-old La Vecchia Dispensa Italian balsamic vinegar, and 66 percent dark chocolate, which was then dusted with freeze-dried strawberry powder.

It wasn't until I knew for certain that I was trading the East Village for the Right Bank that I sampled Rachel's masterpiece: her signature pretzel-covered, sea-salted caramel that had crackly, salty pretzel bits coating the 66 percent cocoa shell and creamy caramel center. "Pop the whole thing in your mouth since it's really liquidy caramel inside," she instructed. I obliged, her eager guinea pig. Sweet-salty had by then become a really popular combination, practiced by everyone from fellow chocolatier Rhonda Kave, who had a small shop, Roni-Sue, in the Lower East Side's Essex Street Market, to Pichet Ong, who had once been Jean-Georges Vongerichten's pastry chef and had gone on to open a succession of bakeries and dessert bars downtown. But Rachel's salty-sweet, one-two punch was absolutely sublime.

"It's the caramel," I gushed. "The texture. It sort of blends both extremes into a big gooey mess of deliciousness that melts on your tongue." She laughed at my professional explanation. "Do you think they have anything like this in Paris?" I asked, licking flicks of caramel left on my fingertips.

"It's probably a little too messy for the French."

"True," I said, while Rachel kindly pointed to her chin, indicating to me that I had a string of caramel there. "I don't know how I'm going to do it," I continued, dotting my face clean. "It's going to be hard being so prim and proper all the time."

She was looking at me, slightly confused. "What are you talking about?"

So I shared my back-and-forth, wait-and-see drama of the past several months, and she started buzzing with excitement. "Oh my god, that's incredible! You have to promise you'll sample every last chocolate in Paris," she said. "No, every last chocolate in France. In *Europe!*" she laughed. Deal, I told her. Fifteen minutes later I said good-bye, buoyed by her enthusiasm and my box of six assorted bonbons.

When I shared the news with AJ, my best friend of twenty-five years, that I had finally received a formal offer, it was a whole different story. I could barely even look at her.

"Seriously?" she choked, both on my news and on a cupcake crumb.

"I know, can you believe it?" We were sitting on a bench outside Billy's Bakery, a Magnolia Bakery spin-off (or rip-off, depending whom you asked, seeing as it was started by an ex-employee of the famed West Village bakery and had the same retro vibe and menu going on, right down to the ratio of Nilla Wafers in the giant vats of creamy banana pudding). The advantage of Billy's was that the *Sex and the City* tour buses didn't stop here, so we weren't confronted with our embarrassing Jersey alter egos. It was also right around the corner from AJ's Chelsea walk-up. We often treated ourselves to a Sunday sweet, either doing new recon for my "Sweet Freak" column or indulging at one of our old faithfuls: City Bakery or here at Billy's. It was our time to catch up on the week and recount the previous night's antics if we had been brave or desperate enough to take on Manhattan's Saturday night scene.

Every time we were at Billy's, AJ got the banana cupcake with cream cheese frosting, a house specialty. I usually felt it my duty to try something new—like the Hello Dolly, a graham-cracker-crusted bar, layered with a tooth-achingly sweet mélange of chocolate chips, pecans, butterscotch, and coconut, perhaps a big old slice of German chocolate cake, or just a modest sugar-dusted snickerdoodle. But today—out of alliance or nervousness, I wasn't sure—I had also ordered a banana cupcake: a wise choice, as it was especially spongy and fresh. I was licking the frosting off my fingertips, watching the stream of yellow cabs zooming down Ninth Avenue, while AJ quietly contemplated my news.

"Wow. No." She sat gazing down at her empty cupcake wrapper, the nutty cake and creamy frosting long gone. Of course I had told her months ago they were looking for writers in Paris and that I was the lead candidate. She had been privy to the blow-by-blow interviewing, negotiating, contract drafting, and waiting over the past few months. But it had taken so long, I don't think either of us thought an official offer letter would ever come through and the move would actually happen.

We'd had a nearly identical conversation earlier that year when AJ interviewed for a job in Venice. In fact, our lives had been eerily parallel since we met on the first day of seventh grade, skinny eleven-year-olds in the Connecticut burbs, sitting near each other during gym class roll call. AJ's family had just moved to town from Iowa. At the time, I didn't know that her giant blue eyes and impossibly friendly attitude were hallmarks of the Midwest. But it wasn't long before we were inseparable and I got to learn other key traits of my corn-fed best friend: loyalty, modesty, and a great desire to have fun, even at the cost of being complete dorks.

Although the past two years in New York had been the only time we lived in the same city at the same time since graduating high school, our friendship never skipped a beat. When AJ decided against the job in Italy, I had breathed a sigh of relief. In our midthirties, we were having the time of our lives being single and crazy together in New York City. Brunching and gallery hopping? Dancing all night? Flirting with men? Check, check, and check. She was my soul sister. We were wondertwins. I couldn't imagine life without her sweet smile, steadfast support, or our shared wardrobe. I know we both felt we dodged a bullet when she took herself out of the running for Venice. But now here I was: preparing to leave New York for Paris.

The last of the burnt-orange leaves had just fallen from the trees, and the city air was clearer and crisper than usual. Every time someone opened the door next to us, the warm baking smells—cinnamon, sugar, nutmeg—deliciously danced by our noses. "That's so great, Aim," she said, changing her tone of voice on the spot. As a leadership management coach, training international C-level executives how to be effective communicators, she was always the best at seeing the positive side to a situation and encouraging others with the right words and genuine support. "You should be so proud of yourself!"

"Yeah, well, there's still a lot of paperwork like the visa application and official stuff like that, so who knows what could still happen? It *is* a luxury brand, after all," I rambled on. "People aren't exactly spending money on logo handbags these days. Without anything signed, I wouldn't be surprised if the opportunity vanished as suddenly as it appeared." My lame rationalizing was beginning to take on a guilty undertone. AJ just looked at me, knowing as well as I did that I would soon be leaving.

As tormented as I had been over the months, deliberating between life in two phenomenal cities, I had gradually begun to want nothing more than to escape New York. It still made me sad to think about leaving my friends and family and comfy life. But it was becoming increasingly clear that a change was for the best. I was thirty-six. Most of my friends were already on their second or third kids and buying matching living-room sets, while I was acting like a twenty-five-year-old, trolling bars at which the male-to-female ratio was about one to three on a good night. The economy was tanking, friends were getting laid off, and the refrain that we should be happy just to have jobs was getting old, to say nothing of depressing—especially since I was being given more and more work on every copywriter's biggest night-mare: health care.

If I stayed in New York, one week would bleed into another. Thirty-six would turn into thirty-seven, and suddenly I would be celebrating my fortieth birthday the same way I celebrated my thirtieth: gathering friends for $15 cocktails at some candlelit bar downtown. Everything was beginning to feel like a threat or a joke, including my once-beloved job. And frankly, I was getting too old to dance all night. I guess the thought of leaving it all behind allowed me to see my life with less-kind eyes. It prompted me to think about my needs in a new way. And I couldn't help but ask: was I really as happy as I had thought I was?

"I'll give it a year," I declared to AJ. "I mean, I can't *not* go; it's like fate or something, right? This opportunity to move to my favorite city in the world—well, besides New York—just walked through my door. I have to try it for at least a year or so."

"I agree—you'd be crazy to pass it up." AJ was always so

thoughtful and insightful, it forced me to be more so too. "What do you want to get out of your time there?"

"Hmmm, good question." I paused, letting my reflections from all the months of waiting and planning surface. "It will be great for my portfolio, working on Louis Vuitton, so there's that. And hopefully I'll get to write about some of my travels while I'm there. Because I definitely want to travel. I want to go to Portugal and Greece, and the south of France, and if I can sell some articles about it, awesome."

"Mmm-hmmm, go on."

"Well, I want to learn French. Maybe take some cooking classes…" I was beginning to get that dreamy feeling that Paris always sparked in me. *This is really going to happen, isn't it?* "I want to explore the city's best sweets and bakeries. And…maybe I'll even fall in love…"

The smile AJ gave me was simultaneously sad and happy. We were entering a new chapter. "Sounds perfect."

—— ✸ ——

In the end, everything fell into place. After five long months of waiting (there it was, the *escargots'* pace again), the papers were signed and I had a one-way ticket in hand. I shipped eight boxes of clothes and shoes, packed my laptop and a suitcase, and steeled myself for the transatlantic flight with Milo—our first trip together. And then, just like that, I was in Paris.

As on all my previous visits, my senses were jolted awake

during my first few hours off the plane. With the limestone architecture and the buzz of scooters, the sound of church bells and the smell of chickens roasting at the *boucheries*, it was an exercise of total indulgence. Alive. I was in Paris, and I felt *alive*!

I ditched my suitcase, unleashed a still-drugged Milo in my dingy hotel room, and started sauntering down the hill in South Pigalle—SoPi as the increasingly hip-to-New-York-acronyms Frenchies called it—wondering how long I could hold out for a warm and melty Nutella street crepe, one of my favorite things to eat in Paris. I was happy to have a cool new neighborhood to explore, seeing as Ogilvy had put me up in a not-so-cool hotel next to the Moulin Rouge. Only four o'clock, and already drunk eighteen-year-olds and retired Japanese tourists spilling out of tour buses like camera-wielding samurais made the neighborhood a minefield.

Beyond the main boulevard were an astounding number of XXX bars that finally gave way to indie music shops and cafés, where, despite the damp March air, people sat on terraces, smoking and talking in small groups. From across the street, I was drawn to a maroon awning: A l'Étoile d'Or. *Hmmm,* I wondered, *qu'est-ce que c'est?* Guidebook stickers plastered the door—badges of legitimacy displayed at restaurants and boutiques around town—so I knew it must be a popular place. But I didn't know I was about to encounter a legend.

I stepped through the door into a little shop of wonders.

The tile floor looked like it had been there for centuries, glass shelves were jammed with colorful tins, and walnut moldings gave a cozy and inviting feel: it was the perfect old-school candy parlor. Best of all, there was chocolate—chocolate everywhere! In the center of the room stood a display case, jammed with petite trays of bonbons. Next to it was a table of stacked bars—Bernachon *tablettes*. Come to find out, this is *très* rare, as hardly anyone outside the Lyonnais bean-to-bar chocolatier, Maurice Bernachon, has the privilege of selling them. There were glass jars flaunting mountains of caramels, suckers, pralined nuts, licorice, and more exquisitely wrapped bars and boxes everywhere I looked. "Bonjour!" a husky voice boomed out of nowhere.

I looked up and saw a woman magically appear from the back room. *Oh my.*

— ✸ —

The name Denise Acabo doesn't mean much to 99 percent of the world's population. But that other one percent is fanatical about her. She's one of the greatest connoisseurs of French chocolate, after all.

It took me a moment to recover, looking at this dame in a tartan plaid skirt and blue vest, with long blonde braids and bifocals and—wait, was that? yes, it was!—the scent of Chanel No. 5. I would later discover Acabo is a cult character in Paris. But that day, she was my secret discovery. For more than her signature look, or even her choco-knowledge, it's her irresistible charm and infectious enthusiasm that reels people in.

Everyone who walks through the doors of her boutique is treated like the most important person in the world. She grabs you by the arm and gushes about her candies: that they're the best of the best and that she's the exclusive carrier in the city. She'll tell you how the cab drivers come in and clean her out of Le Roux caramels and that Japanese tourists fax her magazine articles in which she's appeared. She talks a mile a minute and is as much an entertainer and *theatrice* as a chocolate connoisseur. She could prattle on about *pralinés* for hours—and she will, if you're not careful. I looked at my watch when she paused for a breath and was shocked to see that thirty minutes had passed. It's a shame I could understand only a fraction of what she was saying.

Beyond the language barrier, my head was beginning to spin with all the choices. At the Bernachon table, I stared at all the amazing flavors—espresso, orange, hazelnut, rum raisin—wondering how to choose. But it was simple: I let Denise do it. (And thank goodness. When I unwrapped my *pâte d'amande pistache* chocolate bar back at the hotel, it was like inhaling vats of molten cocoa in a chocolate factory. Delicious without even taking a bite. Between the richness of the 62 percent cacao and the sweet grittiness of Sicilian pistachio paste, I thought I had ascended to chocolate heaven.)

When it came time to selecting bonbons, Denise was

equally strong-willed. After careful consideration, I chose six from the case, but she shot two of them down. "Eh," she started with a look of disdain. It was an expression I would get used to in Paris. "Non, non," she wagged her finger and pointed to another tray instead. "*Celui-ci? Ça, c'est le mieux.*" She wanted to make sure I had the best of the best, so I wound up with a selection from all over the country—Gevrey-Chambertin, Bourges, Lorraine—and from many masters, including Henri Le Roux (salted caramel), Bernard Dufoux (balsamic vinegar truffle), and more from Bernachon (a praline noisette). Even with my impressive haul, there were so many exquisite sweets that I didn't get, including the famed Breton caramels. She's a smart woman, giving you reason to come back.

All of this, six hours into my first day. Walking back up SoPi's hill from A l'Étoile d'Or, this time oblivious to the peepshow bars and pools of tourists, I was glowing from within. I'd have to email Rachel and tell her I was already sampling bonbons. That I'd had my first lesson in Paris—from a fast-talking, kilt-wearing, kooky chocophile. That it looked like my life in Paris was going to be a most delicious learning experience.

In Paris, you can toss a truffle in any direction and hit a world-class chocolatier. (C'est dangereux!) *A l'Étoile d'Or is great, as it pulls in all kinds of French chocolates that are tough to get your hands on, like Bernachon tablettes (bars) from Lyon and Bernard Dufoux bonbons from Burgundy. But some of my favorite city-based chocolatiers include Michel Chaudun, Michel Cluizel, Jacques Genin, and—sigh—Jean-Paul Hévin (in the 7e, 1er, 3e, and 1er, respectively).*

New York has nothing on Paris when it comes to chocolatiers. So I was especially bummed when Rachel shuttered Bespoke in May of 2011 (thank God I made a couple runs for her peanut butter honey squares and pretzel-covered sea-salted caramels before she did). Despite that big loss, there are still several other great artisanal chocolate-makers around town, including Rhonda Kave (Roni-Sue's Chocolates on the Lower East Side), Lynda Stern (Bond Street Chocolates in the East Village), and Kee Ling Tong (Kee's Chocolates in Soho).

— [C H A P T E R   2] —

CUPCAKES — THE COMFORT OF HOME

What can I say about my first weeks in Paris? They. Were. Heaven. I knew such euphoria wasn't sustainable—thirty-six years of experience had taught me that you can always count on a startling crash after the delicious sugar high. So I relished every second of it.

After three weeks in the crummy Pigalle hotel, which skeeved me out to the point where I wouldn't let the blankets touch my face or my bare feet come in contact with the carpeting, I was happy to finally be settling into my new apartment, my new routine, my new life. I was luckier than most. Not only had I come to Paris to live my dream, but somebody else was navigating the nuances of French bureaucracy and footing the bill on my behalf. Ogilvy set me up with a real estate agent who was as tenacious as any New

York broker, orchestrating a single marathon day in which we viewed eleven apartments.

"Operation Dream Pad!" I chirped, driving along the traffic-choked quay overlooking the Seine, on our way from the third apartment in the ninth arrondissement—one of those "up and coming" neighborhoods that was slowly being infiltrated by trendy restaurants and young families—to our next appointment across town in the coveted sixth arrondissement, Paris's Upper East Side, if you will.

I knew the neighborhood profiles thanks mostly to Michael, one of my two friends in Paris. I had met him at a party in New York, one week prior to my Tour du Chocolat vacation. Chatting in a giant Chelsea apartment, The Strokes and Hot Chip thumping so loudly it jiggled my skat, I leaned in toward this River Phoenix–lookalike telling me he lived in Paris. When he went on to specify that he lived in Canal Saint-Martin, I made him promise to show me around the neighborhood, then unknown to me, the next week.

Sure enough, eight days later, I was staring at his back as he took me on my first Vélib' ride, guiding me past the canal's peaked iron bridges and enchanting locks—where Amélie had skipped stones, I excitedly pointed out—to the flat and sprawling Parc de la Villette for a picnic. It was the ultimate romantic summer evening in Paris. Eight o'clock, but the sun still hung in the sky. We had a bottle of rosé, a perfectly crunchy baguette, and a big, stinking hunk of Camembert.

Except there was no romancing.

Not even five minutes into our bike ride, Michael started launching into his exploits of and escapades with Gallic women—code for *Don't get any ideas, missy, I have more sophisticated conquests than you.* Biking home that night, alone, I was disappointed that this storybook rendezvous was wasted on a platonic encounter. But it turns out a friend, not a fling, was the perfect outcome.

All those months when Ogilvy took forever with the contract and I was wavering about moving to Paris, it was Michael whom I emailed, and Michael who responded right away with plenty of Paris persuasion, plus encyclopedic knowledge of expat living. The second, tenth, and eleventh arrondissements were the hippest places to live, he reported. I would have to set aside my own tax fund since France didn't deduct taxes like they do in the States. Do not bring an American DVD player, but buy one in France, with the correct voltage and compatible technology. All the insights and tips he had shared helped me feel more confident in situations like this, driving around with a foreign broker, trying to find the perfect home. And sure enough, by the end of the day, I had narrowed the eleven apartment options down to three contenders, and I got my top choice: a sixth-floor walk-up in the second arrondissement.

Paris is a city of villages, each *quartier*, or neighborhood, its own little universe. The pedestrian Montorgueil quartier I now lived in was, as far as I could tell, one of the city's best—dynamic, central, and young. And with my new apartment's lofty ceilings, exposed wood beams, and views of the Centre Pompidou to the south, Sacré-Coeur to the north, and hundreds of zinc rooftops peppered with terra-cotta chimneys in between, it was like my own little tree house in the city. It suited me and Milo just fine.

The Ogilvy office elicited the same schoolgirl titters from me. A classic *hôtel particulier* right on the Champs-Élysées, I sat overlooking the famed boulevard, beneath sixteen-foot-tall ceilings painted with frescoes of chubby cherubs and fair maidens and dripping with crystal chandeliers. When my boss showed me the rooftop terrace (yes, a *rooftop terrace*, on the *Champs-Élysées*; this was my new *workplace*), I thought I was going to bump my nose against the Eiffel Tower, it was so close.

Remembering how efficient—and fun!—the Vélib's had been the previous summer on my chocolate tour, I relied on them instead of the Métro to get to work every morning. This public bike sharing system has over twenty thousand industrial-looking road bikes stationed at kiosks around the city that are yours to take, so long as you have a daily, weekly, or annual subscription. The bikes have three speeds, little bells for warning heedless pedestrians that you're coming their way, and wire baskets for carrying your bags—or, if you're a super-chic Frenchie, your adorable Jack Russell terrier.

I'd hop on a bike around the corner from my tree house, wind around the delivery trucks in Japantown's narrow streets, and join the cacophony of revving scooters and gushing fountains in Place de la Concorde, where King Louis XVI had been guillotined over two hundred years ago.

The square's grandeur and beauty shocked me anew every day: the scale of the gold-tipped monument, the magnificent dome of Les Invalides in the distance, and, further still, peeking over the sculpted trees, the Eiffel Tower. It was like being part of a moving orchestra—my beating heart and pumping legs trying to match the rhythm of the trucks, buses, taxis, cars, scooters, and pedestrians swooshing through the motorway.

Then I'd peel off to Avenue Gabriel and give my silent respects while pedaling by the U.S. embassy and President Sarkozy's residence, admire the grand dames strolling the sidewalks in the tony eighth arrondissement, and then finish my ride. I parked the Vélib' in the closest kiosk to the office, which just so happened to be outside the grand and historical tea salon with some of the best cakes and macarons in the city: Ladurée.

Two mornings a week, I went to the office early to meet Josephine, my French tutor, arranged by Ogilvy. With her perpetually perspiring brow, rosy cheeks, and powdery perfume smell, she reminded me of my third-grade teacher, Miss Dickus. Or maybe it was just because I felt like a schoolgirl, taking lessons again. The office was always quiet at 8:30 a.m., save for the cleaning crew's vacuums, giving us ninety minutes of conversational and grammatical lessons—well, less the fifteen minutes that Josephine always reserved for complaining about the weather, the Métro, being overworked, or a combination of all three.

As keen as I was to learn French, always completing my homework and paying close attention to Josephine's perfectly planned lessons, I soon learned that language is not my strong suit. But still, I did what I could and started a list of handy slang, picked up from colleagues and fashion websites, that was almost more essential than the *passé composé* and "er," "ir," and "re" verbs. I learned words and expressions like *ça marche* (that works, or, okay) and *ça craint* (that sucks); *talons hauts* (high heels) and *baskets* (trendy sneakers); *malin* (wicked smart or cool) and *putain* (literally, a whore, but used as an expression of frustration, anger, or awe). I learned that the French like to *manger les mots*, creating shorthand like *bon app* for *bon appétit*, *d'acc* instead of *d'accord*, and *resto* rather than *restaurant*. After years of being on cruise control, there was now something new to learn every day.

It was almost stupid how picture-perfect my new life was. The whole thing felt like a cliché, even to me. There I was, in the fashion capital of the world, working on one of the most recognizable and successful luxury brands. One day, as I wandered around the Louis Vuitton flagship store on the Champs-Élysées—part of my *professional obligation*, for God's sake—I literally pinched myself. Was this for real? Why was I there? How was I suddenly living in Paris, among the €2,000 evening dresses and 98 percent dark chocolate bars? Was it fate? I didn't have the answers, but I smiled with giddiness, hopelessly in love with the entire world.

—— ✸ ——

As smiley as I was, my enthusiasm was not infectious.

"Avez-vous du pain complét ce soir?" I asked, waltzing into "my" *boulangerie* one evening for some whole wheat bread. Surely, the squat, bespectacled madam behind the counter recognized me by now? I had been coming in for weeks, demonstrating not only my loyalty to her business, but also my appreciation for French culture. Each visit, I requested a different kind of bread: a round and rustic *boule au levain*; *pain bûcheron*, kneaded and roasted to crunchy perfection; the *baguette aux céréales* with its delightful mix of sesame, sunflower, millet, and poppy seeds. It was my duty to understand France's abundance of deliciousness.

"Non, madame." Blank face. She wasn't budging. So what if I ate whole wheat? I was still *une étrangère* in her eyes, not a Frenchie. I felt a momentary pang of defeat from her indifference. With other recent roadblocks due to my inability to decipher the deposit forms at the bank, the milk labels at the grocery store, the processes (or lack thereof) at the office, and, generally, just what the hell everyone was saying to me, being unceremoniously shut down was a feeling that was beginning to edge in on my bliss more and more often. It was after seven o'clock and the shelves were nearly depleted.

I had a new bread addiction for which I needed a fix, *tout de suite*. Suddenly, as if my guardian angel and Houdini had been conspiring in the kitchen, a young man dusted in flour appeared from behind a curtain with a cylindrical basket of fresh baguettes. My smile returned. "Pas grave," I declared. "Une demi-baguette, s'il vous plaît!"

The woman pulled one of the golden specimens from the basket—the man sauntering back behind the curtain from where he magically came—deftly sliced it in two, and slipped one half in a paper sack—*une demi-baguette,* perfect for the single girl. "Avec ceci?" she asked in that French sing-song way, drawing out the "ce" and especially the "ci," peering over her wire-rims. The French were always pushing a little more on you.

"Non, c'est tout," I replied, happy for this little exchange that made me—almost—feel like I belonged here. I grabbed the change she plunked on the counter and turned on my heel. "Merci, madame!" I bellowed, careful to enunciate each syllable like the good French student I was.

"Merci à vous," she replied, the ingrained French *politesse* kicking in. "Bonne soirée."

Out on the sidewalk, in the damp April air, my smile

erupted again. Through the thin *boulangerie* paper, I could feel the warmth of the baguette, making it irresistibly squishy in my hand. It was one of God's gifts to the world, I had decided: French bread, fresh from the oven. There was no way I was waiting until I was back at my tree house to indulge. I tore a piece of the baguette off, trailing crumbs behind me, and crunched into it. The crust resisted for a moment and then the crisp outside revealed the doughy, dense, and spongy inside. How could four little ingredients—flour, water, yeast, and salt—produce something so otherworldly? I stopped on the sidewalk, my eyes rolling in the back of my head as I chewed very, very slowly, savoring the baguette's flavor.

I opened my eyes and a girl smoking outside a bar was staring at me. I had become infatuated with French women, more so than the slim-hipped, effeminate men, developing girl-crushes daily. Their lips were always painted perfectly in magenta or tomato red. Their eyeliner was at once retro and modern, like Brigitte Bardot's. And their hair was always disheveled but perfectly so, as if they'd just had a romp in bed. They were sexy, stylish, and gorgeous. I felt horribly dull with my brown hair and *au naturel* makeup—both pretty much unchanged since the day I graduated from college. Whenever I was around a particularly *jolie femme*, I could hear Edith Wharton whispering in my ear, "Compared with the women of France, the average American woman is still in kindergarten." *Touché, Edith.*

The girl outside the bar was in Parisian uniform: slim jeans tucked into short cowboy booties, a leather coat hanging off her thin frame, and an oversized scarf, which, like her hair, was effortlessly yet studiously haphazard. I smiled. I felt a bonding moment between us, her looking at me, me looking at her, just two girls of the world. But she just pulled an impossibly long drag from her cigarette, tossed it in the gutter, and subtly rolled her eyes before disappearing back inside the bar. Paris was cool; apparently, I was not.

In fact, I knew I wasn't. Edith Wharton wasn't the only thing I had been reading. I had been dipping into all the tomes about living in and adjusting to France and I suddenly recalled a small but important gem. That in America, everyone smiles at strangers—your neighbors, the checkout girl, the cop giving you a ticket for doing 45 in a 35-mile-per-hour zone—as a friendly, pacifying gesture. In France, the only people who smile at strangers are mentally retarded.

I found the insight so ridiculous and funny and, if I were any example, apparently true. I laughed out loud and continued down the street with my baguette, looking "touched" for sure.

---- ✳ ----

As American as I appeared with my big, dorky grin on the outside, I was beginning to understand—a deep, in-my-bones understanding—the French appreciation for food.

Nobody at the office deigned to eat lunch at their desks as we had habitually done in New York. Little pockets of colleagues broke off and ceremoniously ate together. A small group of twenty-something-year-old women would have their meals, packed from home, in the office kitchen, while most of the guys went out to local cafés. I tried not to mind not having anyone to lunch with yet, and quickly learned not to "eeeet in zeee streeeeet," as one of my colleagues caught me doing one day—a true faux pas to the always-proper Parisians. Instead, I took advantage of the break to explore the neighborhood.

Offices cleared out and boutiques were closed from noon until 2:00 p.m., while the sidewalks, *boulangeries*, and bistros came alive. The French got so much pleasure out of shopping for and eating food every day. Mealtime was sacred. Food was celebrated. It wasn't forbidden or an enemy for which the French needed gym memberships, cabbage soup diets, or magic powders and pills (though I did have my suspicions about French women and laxatives).

What's more, there were entire shops devoted to singular foods: stocky, pot-bellied men in wader boots and white lab coats stood outside *poissonneries*, even in the coldest weather, showcasing filets of the catch of the day, while other boutiques offered scores of colorful and alluring tins of foie gras. On Sunday afternoons, so many people stood in line at the *fromageries*, *boulangeries*, and boucheries that I made a game out of counting them. How wonderful that families were stocking up for their big Sunday *repas*, doing all their food shopping the day of the meal, at small neighborhood businesses. Back home, we'd load up a giant grocery cart once a week at a superstore, and then shelve the packaged goods in the pantry until memory or hunger called them forth. Fresh, local, and delicious was not the marketing mantra du jour in Paris. It's just the way it was.

Before choosing my apartment, I hadn't really understood why Michael was so gung ho about the second arrondissement. My previous visits to Paris had given me the impression that it was more commercial and touristy than residential and charming. But I soon discovered that my neighborhood was one of the biggest foodie meccas in the city, anchored by the four-block pedestrian stretch of rue Montorgueil. By my count, it had two cheese shops (*fromageries*), four produce markets (*marchés*), four butchers (*boucheries*), one of which was devoted to chickens (*un rotisserie*), a fish market (*poissonnerie*), four chocolate boutiques (*chocolatiers*), an ice cream shop (*un glacier*), six bakeries (*boulangeries*), four wine stores (*caves au vin*), an Italian specialty shop, and a giant market filled with heaps of spices, dried fruits, nuts, and grains that were sculpted into neat domes and sold by the gram. There was even a store devoted just to olive oils. And all of these were interspersed between no fewer than a dozen cafés, a couple florists (*fleuristes*), and myriad *tabacs*, where weathered old men bought their Lotto tickets and drank beer with their mutts and neighbors.

Walking that stretch of food paradise that was my new neighborhood, which I made sure to do at least once a day, made all my senses tingle: produce—towering stacks of purple-flecked artichokes and pyramids of pert, shiny clementines—was displayed like kinetic sculptures, changing shape as the day went on and the inventory decreased. The pungency of ripe, stinky cheeses duked it out with the smell of savory fat drippings falling from chickens that roasted on spits into pans of peeled potatoes below. And even though I hadn't eaten red meat in over ten years, I still took the time to peer into the *charcuteries*, marveling at the coils of sausages and terrines of pâtés and how wonderfully they were displayed. The food was treated so respectfully that I had no choice but to genuflect. It was glorious.

And then there were the pâtisseries and *boulangeries*. While I had arrived in Paris with the names of only two friends scribbled on a scrap of paper, I had a carefully researched, very thorough two-page spreadsheet of must-try pâtisseries. I got right to work.

Within weeks, I had explored all the *boulangeries* and pâtisseries near me and quickly became obsessed with Stohrer's *pain aux raisins*. Come to find out, Stohrer wasn't just the prettiest and most charming bakery on rue Montorgueil, but it also had the most illustrious roots, having been started in

1730 by King Louis XV's royal pâtissier, Nicolas Stohrer. I'd never been interested in *pain aux raisins* before, always preferring a rich and melty *pain au chocolat*, a rectangular croissant hiding two *batonettes* of chocolate inside, to something with ho-hum raisins. But one morning when I saw Stohrer's pastry pinwheels, filled generously with *crème pâtissière* and riddled with raisins looking especially puffy and inviting, I gave it a try. It was still slightly warm. It was sweeter than I expected. I was smitten.

Inspired, I set off for other *boulangeries* and pâtisseries in the city. There was Les Petits Mitrons, a cute little pink pâtisserie in Montmartre that specialized in tarts: chocolate-walnut, chocolate-pear, apple-pear, straight-up chocolate, straight-up apple, apricot, peach, rhubarb, fig, *fruits-rouges*, strawberry-cream, mixed fruit, and on and on. From there, I ventured east to one of the city's only other hilly quartiers, Belleville, searching for the best croissant in Paris.

As I pedaled through the working-class neighborhood on my way to La Flute Gana, a *boulangerie* I had read about, I had a happy jolt, suddenly remembering one of my favorite all-time French movies: *The Triplets of Belleville*. The image of those three crazy animated ladies, snapping their fingers, swinging their *derrières*, and singing on stage evoked such unadulterated glee, which was matched once I arrived at the *boulangerie* and bit into my long-anticipated croissant: a gazillion little layers of fine, buttery pastry dough, coiled and baked together in soft-crunchy perfection.

Every weekend, my sweet explorations continued this way. On the chichi shopping stretch of rue Saint-Honoré, I indulged in Jean-Paul Hévin's Choco Passion, a rich nutty and fruity cake with a flaky praline base, dark chocolate ganache, and chocolate mousse whipped with tart passion fruit. In the Marais, a neighborhood alternatively known for its Jewish roots, gay pride, and fantastic shopping, I sampled Pain de Sucre's juicy and herbaceous rhubarb and rosemary tart. I discovered that the wonderful 248-year-old, lost-in-time candy and chocolate shop in the ninth arrondissement, À la Mère de Famille, carried dried pineapple rings, a treat I had been obsessed with for three decades (don't ask; I think it's a texture thing). And I started developing a new weakness for Haribo gummies, available at any old crummy supermarket.

As I cruised by the Jardin du Luxembourg, just beginning to burst in an array of spring greens, with a belly full of matcha-flavored ganache from the nearby Japanese pâtisserie Sadaharu Aoki, I rationalized that pastry hunting was a very good way for me to get to know my new hometown. But as I continued Vélib'ing around town and eating up Parisian sweets, no one could have been more surprised than me to discover that cupcakes were now storming the Bastille.

—— ✳ ——

I think it's safe to say that by 2007 or 2008, cupcakes trumped apple pie as the all-American iconic sweet. And I witnessed their rise to sugary stardom firsthand in New York.

When I moved to the city in 2001, the trend was just taking off. At the time, I was also on the brink. I was almost thirty years old, excited and hopeful for all that might be. After spending my twenties in San Francisco, much of it in a seven-year relationship that ultimately wasn't "the one," and in an advertising career in which I always felt the desire to write for a glossy magazine tugging at me, I had moved back east to pursue my dreams. I had proven to myself that I could be an advertising copywriter. Now I wanted to be a New York writer, who had a byline in the *Times* and lunched at Union Square Café. The world was my proverbial oyster. But, since I don't like briny delicacies, I considered the world my cupcake instead: sweet and inviting, familiar yet new, indulgent but only modestly so. And just when I thought I had tasted every possibility—yellow cake with chocolate frosting, chocolate with vanilla buttercream, peanut butter cup—a new cupcakery would open, and there would be a whole new inspired menu to bite into.

As I blazed my personal cupcake trail, Carrie Bradshaw and Miranda Hobbes sent the whole world into a cupcake tizzy. Once those two sat chomping into their pink frosted cupcakes, dishing on Aidan, in the third season of *Sex and the City*, the *petits gâteaux* became inescapable. And

Magnolia Bakery, the location of their sweet moment, went from modestly successful to insanely popular to polarizing and reviled.

Magnolia was started in July of 1996 by two friends, Allysa Torey and Jennifer Appel. On a quiet corner in the West Village, they launched a genius concept: old-fashioned baked goods—perfectly frosted three-layer cakes, freshly baked pies dusted with cinnamon, fudgy brownies, and tart lemon squares—served up in an adorable, wholesome space that could have been Betty Crocker's own kitchen. But as the business soared, the women's relationship soured. Three years after opening, they split, with Allysa running the original bakery solo, and Jennifer moving to Midtown to open Buttercup, a bakery with virtually the same exact menu and aesthetic. Both of them churned out pretty pastel cupcakes, and the city ate them up.

Buttercup, probably because of its unsexy midtown location, fared just okay, but Magnolia went gangbusters. The more popular it became, the more people loved to hate it. The staff was infamously snippy. The lines, which grew so long they snaked out the door and around the corner, started annoying the neighbors. Then the *Sex and the City* tour buses rolled in and put everyone over the top. The bakery and its cupcakes became synonymous with Carrie Bradshaw wannabes, tottering in their heels and not caring about on whose front stoop they were dropping their frosting-laced wrappers.

The cupcakes themselves were hit or miss, love 'em or hate 'em. While cake flavors were the standard yellow, chocolate, and red velvet, and generally tasty, it was the frosting that sent everyone spiraling. It was über sweet, pastel-colored, dotted with vibrant sprinkles, and swirled on in abundance. These little cakes became the downtown must-have accessory, as fashionable as the T-shirts and coin purses Marc Jacobs was peddling across the street.

Meanwhile, other cupcakeries were popping up all over Manhattan. A near Magnolia replica turned up in Chelsea when a former bakery manager jumped ship to open his Americana bakeshop, Billy's (the one AJ and I frequented). Two Buttercup employees similarly ventured downtown to the Lower East Side and opened Sugar Sweet Sunshine, expanding into new flavors like the Lemon Yummy, lemon cake with lemon buttercream, and the Ooey Gooey, chocolate cake with chocolate almond frosting. *Dee*-licious.

Other bakeries opted for their own approach. A husband-and-wife team opened Crumbs, purveyor of five-hundred-calorie softball-sized juggernauts, in outrageous flavors like Chocolate Pecan Pie and Coffee Toffee, topped with candy shards and cookie bits. There were also mini cupcakes in wacky flavors like chocolate chip pancake and peanut butter and jelly from Baked by Melissa and Kumquat's more gourmet array like lemon-lavender and maple-bacon.

Revered pastry chefs also got in on the action. After

opening ChikaLicious, the city's first dessert bar, Chika Tillman launched a take-out spot across the street that offered Valrhona chocolate buttercream-topped cupcakes. And Pichet Ong, a Jean-Georges Vongerichten alum and dessert bar and bakery rock star, attracted legions of loyal fans—no one more than myself—to his West Village bakery, Batch, with his carrot salted-caramel cupcake.

By 2009, dozens of bakeries vied for the title of Best Cupcake in New York. There were literally hundreds of flavors, sizes, and styles; they were sold with different philosophies, and sometimes even rules applied (no more than six cupcakes for you, missy!). Surely, the city could only stomach so much sugar? A cupcake crash was inevitable, though it took years longer than I ever expected.

—— ✳ ——

It had been almost two months since I had arrived in Paris. I still hadn't experienced a free-falling sugar crash, though I *was* beginning to feel a little schizophrenic. One minute, I'd be ecstatically doing the cha-cha in my tree house, and the next, I'd be cursing the six flights of stairs that kicked my ass to get up there. After a day of being unable to conceal my big American smile, someone would be rude to me and my chin would start trembling with hurt. Which led to doubt, which led to me feeling like a seven-year-old being ostracized on the playground, doomed never to fit in. I'd reprimand myself:

Buck up! Get over it! You're living your dream, you have no right to be sad or feel sorry for yourself!

But after a couple months away from home, my confidence was taking a beating in the face of so many changes and challenges. It was a salty-sweet mélange of excitement and dread. Bliss and dismay. Giddiness and loneliness. I had already gotten myself right back up from the ground after flying over the handlebars of a Vélib' one time, but on a Saturday afternoon, after having fallen down the stairs of a boutique, horribly embarrassing myself, butchering my knee and, worst of all, ruining my brand new Robert Clergerie *talons hauts*, I limped home, confidence shattered along with tough-girl façade. I called AJ.

"Hello?" a very sleepy voice answered. I looked at my clock and only then did the math. *Merde.* It was 9:00 a.m. in New York.

"Hi. Did I wake you?"

"No, no," AJ valiantly said from across the ocean. "Don't worry about it. How are you?" I could hear her getting up. She never would have ignored a call from me. Even though I relied on her altruism, it still astounded me.

"Mmmm…I'm okay…" I found myself hedging, for some reason not wanting to say anything negative about Paris or my feeling vulnerable, even though it's why I had called.

"Aim, hold on, just a sec, sorry." I heard AJ covering the mouthpiece, followed by muffled conversation. Hmmmm…

she wasn't alone? I knew she had started dating someone right around the time I moved, but I'd be surprised if he was already spending the night. Come to think of it, she had been very mum about men lately, which, according to my knowledge of her dating behavior, developed from two-plus decades of experience, meant it was nothing serious. She would have been sharing blow-by-blow info if there was someone worth talking about. Turns out, I was wrong.

"Who was *that*?" I asked when she returned to the phone.

"Hold on," and I heard the door click behind her. A moment later, she was revealing that it was Mitchell, the very same guy she started seeing when I moved to Paris—and they were indeed getting serious. In fact, they were all but inseparable.

I was, well, shell-shocked—which at least distracted me from my now-throbbing knee. I hadn't even remembered this guy's name, for crying out loud, and he was suddenly important in my best friend's life? "So what makes him different? What have you guys been doing together? What's the deal?" I asked quick-fire, as if I were interviewing her for an article.

"Well, he's just pretty amazing, you know? He's smart and edgy. He's cool. And he's from the Midwest, so we have a lot of shared values, which is becoming more important to me." As AJ went on, I felt like I had entered a time warp. *Wait a minute*, I thought. *In the time I've been trying to decipher my cable box in French, she's met someone edgy and cool who she feels compatible with?*

Sure, I was also having a love affair—with a city. But AJ was smitten with a man. I could hear it in her voice. And while I was happy for my best friend, I also started feeling sorry for myself. After weeks of exerting so much effort and trying so hard to acclimate, I was tired. Frustrated. Lonely and uncertain. I had Michael and was becoming friendly with another writer at Ogilvy, but these weren't friends I could call in this vulnerable state and hash through my feelings over cocktails. A fierce wave of alienation nearly knocked me over when AJ and I hung up. *What was I doing here?* I looked around my tree house, which suddenly felt foreign. I needed a taste of home, I decided, no matter how small.

— ✳ —

Right before my arrival in Paris, two sisters—Rebecca and Maggie Bellity—opened Cupcakes & Co. in the eleventh arrondissement. They had traveled throughout the States and been inspired by the cupcake trend that had spread across the country. When they returned to Paris in the fall of 2008, they set up what was then Paris's sole cupcake bakery, making a name for themselves by not only featuring these funny little foreign treats, but also touting natural and organic ingredients, another hot foodie trend. As I coasted on a Vélib' through the unfamiliar backstreets behind the Bastille, searching for this itty-bitty spot I had read about, I was filled with anticipation. Would their cupcakes be as good as those in the States?

When I arrived, the afternoon sun was spilling through the picture window onto the bakery's one table. The space was tiny. The menu, however, was not. Choosing between five or ten cupcake flavors, the number most New York bakeries offered, was hard enough. But Cupcakes & Co. had over twenty varieties, and they all sounded heavenly: coffee and hazelnut, poppy seed with orange cream cheese frosting, vanilla bourbon cake with glazed figs and pine nuts. *Miam*, my new favorite word popped into my head—the French equivalent of *yum*.

I stood like a clueless American tourist, cross-referencing the descriptions on the chalkboard menu with the pretty creations in the display case. There were many unfamiliar words—*fondant chocolat* and *ganache au beurre*—which I filed away for future reference. Face scrunched in concentration, I tortured myself making this very important decision. While I knew a cupcake would momentarily transport me back to New York, the connection went deeper and further than that. It took me back to when I was an awkward third grader, alone in the world for the very first time.

—— ✳ ——

I was eight when my parents got divorced and my mom shepherded me and my older brother, Chris, from our home in Hartford, Connecticut, to the shoreline where she grew up. When we left my neighborhood friends and our grand old house, I cried with heartache and disbelief. What would I do without my two best friends right next door? How could I live without the big Douglas fir outside my bedroom window? Who would make runs to the drugstore for strawberry Charleston Chews and nutty Whatchamacallits with me? Now when the yellow bus dropped me off from school, I had to unlock the front door of our raised ranch with my own key that I hyperconsciously carried in my front pocket. I was a latchkey kid. For the first time in my life, I was all alone.

But if the house was empty every day when I got home from school, at least the bread drawer was always full. Devil Dogs and Twinkies, Ho Hos and Chocodiles, Chips Ahoy and Nutter Butters, Oreos and Fudge Stripes, Scooter Pies and Pinwheels, Entenmann's danishes and Pillsbury pastries, brownies and blondies, chocolate cake and carrot cake, Linzer torts and cherry pie, coffee cake and jelly doughnuts, jelly beans and licorice whips, Swedish fish and gummy worms, M&Ms and bridge mix, Kit Kats and Twix, ice cream and popsicles, Fruit Loops and Cinnamon Toast Crunch, Pepperidge Farm and Keebler, Hostess and Drake's, Mars and Cadbury…

All those years after the divorce, there was a Technicolor parade of sweets masquerading as my companions. How could I not cling to and love them? They never disappointed me. They had the magical power to console and cheer me up. They made life celebratory and fun. Especially a cream-filled Hostess CupCake.

Ripping open the cellophane package of those cupcakes was like unwrapping a little gift. It gave me a rapturous—albeit fleeting—diversion from my dull, empty life. With the lonesome shuffling between Mom and Dad, whom Chris and I visited every other weekend, I *deserved* those little treats, dammit! I focused first on the frosting, peeling the waxy layer off the cake in one sheaf, folding it in half, and savoring the gritty-smooth texture when I bit into it. Then came the sugary implosion of the cake's faux-cream center. I made each cupcake last for eight or nine delicious bites. Even though we always had sweets in the house, money was tight, and we were on a budget. If I were to devour the whole box of cupcakes, I would have nothing to look forward to the next day. Or the day after that. I knew to ration my Hostess CupCakes so I could always have a taste of comfort, even when money, attention, and hope were sparse.

To this day, a cupcake can make me feel like all is well in the world.

— ✳ —

The longer I analyzed Cupcake & Co.'s menu, the more my taste buds perked up. Even better than feeling the cartwheels of anticipation in my belly, my spirits started lifting. Finally, I felt ready to make a decision: I chose the Scheherazade, an irresistible-sounding combination of pistachio cake with cream cheese frosting and a raspberry center, topped with a generous sprinkling of crushed pistachios and one perfect raspberry. I've always loved raspberries but since arriving in Paris had a newfound passion for pistachios, which were included in so many delectable desserts and pastries, either whole or ground with sugar into delicious marzipan.

Feeling conspicuous in the petite bakery, I thanked the lady and took my loot to the community park across the street. The square's center was filled with planted shrubs and trees, so I chose one of the three narrow paths slicing through and traversed to the other side, where I sat on a slotted bench beneath a cherry blossom tree in full bloom. There was barely anyone sharing the park with me—just a heavy-set African woman reading the newspaper and an older gentleman in a tie, hooked up to an oxygen machine, just sitting, enjoying the day. I eyed my Parisian specimen. The lining was sturdier than those back home; more of a paper cup with a thick lip than a wrapper. But otherwise, with its fastidiously swirled frosting and sprinkling of pistachio pieces, it looked like it could have been from one of New York's best bakeries. *Here goes nothing*, I thought.

I bit into my first Parisian cupcake. The cake was moist. The raspberry center was bright and jammy. The frosting was thick—not too much so—and savory more than sweet, the cream cheese adding just the right hint of sourness. I took a second bite and a third. It was an unforgivably delicious combination of flavors, textures, and surprises. Relief flooded me.

So there I was, alone again. But this time I was in Paris. I had come a long way from a lonely eight-year-old and a newbie New Yorker trying to find her way. I had so much to be grateful for and even more to look forward to. Nearly three decades after my love affair with cupcakes began, I sat deconstructing a small piece of cake, amazed that even now it could instill such peace, happiness, and a belief that everything was going to be okay.

New Yorkers talk out of both sides of their mouths—even when they're cramming them full of fist-sized bits of cake slathered in buttercream frosting. As "over" cupcakes as everyone purportedly is, you can still find them on practically every block. Beyond Magnolia, Buttercup, Billy's, and Sugar Sweet Sunshine, which all have similar sugary repertoires, check out Butter Lane, The Spot, and Tu-Lu's in the East Village; Out of the Kitchen and Sweet Revenge in the West Village; Babycakes on the Lower East Side; Baked by Melissa in Soho; Lulu in Chelsea; and Two Little Red Hens on the Upper East Side. Or just stand on a street corner and eventually they'll come to you—cupcake trucks, like CupCake Stop, are also now prolific.

Is Paris far behind? It's doubtful. The longer I was there, the more cupcakeries sprouted up like pretty springtime crocuses. In addition to Cupcakes & Co., there is Berko, an American-style French bakery with outposts in the tourist-friendly Marais and Montmartre quartiers, serving circus-like flavors such as banana and Nutella, tarte tatin, and Oreo. Across town in Saint-Germain, Synie's Cupcakes takes the elegant route with chocolate ganache, lemon ginger, and dulce de leche with

sea salt. Cupcakes are even infiltrating traditional boulangeries *(such as the seventh arrondissement's Moulin
de la Vierge), gelaterias (Il Gelato in Saint-Germain),
and Anglo-American eateries (H.A.N.D. in the 1er).
Throwing a soirée or just feeling especially gluttonous?
Batches of custom-order cupcakes are gladly supplied
by Sugar Daze and Sweet Pea Baking, two American
bakers who have been supplying Parisians with frosting-
topped treats for years.*

CHAPTER 3

STICK-TO-YOUR-TEETH HOT COCOA

*Y*ou wouldn't know it from the hyperactive social life I'd left behind in New York, but I've always been a closet introvert. After my parents' divorce, I spent so much time alone. If Chris and I weren't parked on the couch, watching back-to-back episodes of *The Brady Bunch* or hours of Billy Idol, the Go-Go's, and Bananarama videos on the new cable channel called MTV, then I'd lock myself in my room and focus on my new passions: journaling and writing poetry. I became good at withdrawing inside my head.

After years of being on the go in New York, I was once again relishing peace and solitude in Paris; I was having a relationship with *me*. I could binge on *Top Chef* for hours (and, all too frequently, did), cocoon myself in a warm café with a juicy novel, or take off on a Vélib' for a pastry-sampling mission any time I wanted. Having so much freedom was almost as seductive as the city itself.

That said, after a couple months as a foreigner, with no post-work happy hours, no groups of girls gathered for cocktails, no delicious *tête-à-têtes*, no titillating first dates, and not being able to just let loose in a gush of words—in *English*—I was practically ready to explode with my unexpressed thoughts, observations, joys, and frustrations. I was hungry for conversation and companionship. When friends and family started making plans to visit me, I practically wept with relief.

— ✸ —

I knew the upcoming girls weekend I was planning with AJ and our three other best friends was going to be brilliant. From the time of bad perms and acid-wash jeans, AJ, Julie, Elisa, and Meredith were my soul sisters. We had all graduated from the same high school two decades earlier. We'd been through first dates and heartbreaks, driver's ed, and art history exams. When everyone scattered to different states for college, we sent each other off with teary good-byes and mixed tapes of Cat Stevens, Van Morrison, and the Indigo Girls. Many years and miles later, we were just as close—and just as cheesy.

Meredith, Julie, and Elisa were married with two kids. But, impressively, it didn't stop them from saddling their husbands with child care duties for a long weekend every year so we could all get together. We made a point of doing getaway weekends as often as we could, and my living in Paris was the perfect excuse for a spring fling.

But while I was researching good restaurants and bars for the girls weekend, my mom and stepfather became my maiden visitors to Paris. My brother Chris and his family lived just a couple hours north in London, where he worked for a British consulting firm. Now that I was in Paris, it was the perfect excuse for Mom and Bob—two typical, conservative all-Americans—to visit their grandkids in one world-class European capital before making their way to another. So early one Friday morning in late April, instead of Vélib'ing to work, I took the Métro four stops to Gare du Nord and awaited my first visitors.

Being rush hour, the station was abuzz with commuters, travelers, and—pigeons. People talk about the minefields of dog poop in Paris and warn you about the pickpockets on the Métro, but they never breathe a word about how insane the pigeons are. Every time I sat on a park bench or café terrace, the filthy creatures had no qualms about hopping around my feet and hovering dangerously close to my head. When I was Vélib'ing, they'd play chicken, daring me to run them over before ascending in a dirty flap of wings at the very last minute, making me wobble precariously on my two wheels. They even dive-bombed me. Parisian pigeons, I was finding, were the most reckless and infuriating in the world.

There were scores of them now, sending skeevy shivers down my back as I paced below the arrivals board. I wanted to clap and scatter them in the open-air train station, but the thought of all those dirty wings fluttering around my head kept my childish impulses in check. Instead, I mentally reviewed the itinerary for the four days ahead, keeping one eager eye on the big clock and one wary eye on the flying rats.

And then in the sea of smart-looking Europeans deboarding a Eurostar train, I saw them. Mom, a sliver of a thing, appeared even smaller bobbing along in her long cardigan, draped scarf, and oversized shoulder bag. Next to her, Bob, who could play Kris Kringle's brother with his jolly belly, silver-gray beard, and blue eyes, dwarfed her and most of the people around them. Ordinarily, I would have been embarrassed by their excessive waving, giggling, and other displays of Americanism, but as they rushed down the platform, my mom hopping up and down like a six-year-old, it just made me happy. I actually found myself swallowing a lump in my throat.

They had never even been overseas before. Their typical vacations, which were few and far between, usually entailed driving eight hours from their home in western New York to see me in Manhattan or other family in Connecticut. And being devotees of Fox News, I knew leaving U.S. soil (especially for France, *zut alors!*) made them more than a little anxious. That they had flown thousands of miles into foreign territory, changed planes, dealt with security, and gone through customs was nothing short of epic. And not only had they done all that, but after visiting Chris in London, they had just "chunnelled" to Paris by themselves. I was so proud of them.

"Oh, honey," my mom cried, galloping over to wrap me in a hug. Even though I had five inches and twenty pounds on her, there was no one whose arms made me feel more secure.

"Hi, Aim!" Bob, sporting a bright red Izod under his tracksuit jacket, joined the hug. Ah, home! Comfort! Love! At the Gare du Nord in Paris. It was fantastically surreal.

As relieved as I was that they had successfully navigated the international travels, that wasn't the end of my anxiety. I'd be lying if I said I wasn't nervous about exploring Paris with them. Back home, they drive half a mile to pick up a carton of milk, and having a lunch date is considered a major outing. Would they collapse after an hour of walking? Would they need to rest every five minutes? I saw they had their spiffy new sneakers on; were they also—horror of horrors—packing fanny packs?

It was more than the physical stuff, though. I felt as if I had a lot to prove on this trip. Having them here made me hyperaware of my attachment to Paris. I felt this weird ownership, as though I was personally responsible for everything from the dour weather to the magic of the Seine at sunset. A cocktail of pride and angst mixed inside of me: I felt giddy and protective. I yearned to share everything with these two virgin travelers but also felt the compulsion to claim it as my own. This beautiful place was a mystery to them, but it was my whole world now.

I wanted to show them, especially my mom, that I *belonged* in Paris. Despite her chin-up Yankee resignation that her only daughter had moved overseas at an age when she should have been bearing grandchildren, I knew it pained her. She would never say anything to make me feel guilty. In fact, Mom never uttered a word that wasn't supportive of me and my choices. She was my biggest cheerleader. Still, I knew she loved my brother's kids, my adorable niece and nephew, to pieces and wanted more grandchildren. She wanted me to have kids so I could have that whole pregnancy and parenthood experience and know what being a mother *felt* like. And I, in turn, needed her to understand how I felt in Paris. Why I kept coming back to this city. Why it was in my blood and bones. Paris never let me forget the beauty, magic, and wonder I experienced when I first went as a college student, sixteen years earlier. Now it was time to justify my love.

— ✳ —

"Wow." We were hauling ourselves up the six flights to my tree house. I didn't know if Mom's utterance was the full extent of her shock at my steep and winding staircase, or if she was just too winded to say anything else. Six flights was no joke, and I felt a little bad, dragging them up, up, up. But I also had a special, masochistic love for my daily climb; along with the Vélib's, I attributed it to keeping my butt relatively the same size since arriving, despite my regular pastry binges.

Meanwhile, Bob, lugging the suitcases, had to stop on every other landing to huff and puff and laugh at the inanity. This was certainly a lot more rigorous than using the garage door opener and parking within inches of their front door. By the time we all made it upstairs and threw down the luggage, none of us relished the idea of turning right around. But there was a city outside—an entire beautiful, romantic, wonderfully delicious city out there—waiting to be explored. So I quickly showed them the views of the Centre Pompidou and Sacré-Coeur, which prompted more "wows"; they gave Milo a little American love, which elicited some happy purring; and then we set out together to embrace Paris.

—— ✹ ——

"Oh my god, it's gorgeous." My mom was already reaching for her camera.

"Oh, geez, Mom, that's bona fide Paris skank." We were strolling from rue Montorgueil toward the Seine, and she was taking a photo of Les Halles. Decades ago, it would have been worthy of a picture, for sure. It had once been the city's central market, where, beneath glass and iron structures, fish-mongers, butchers, and farmers from the country convened to sell their goods. Now it was a loathsome hub of neon chain stores, where loud and aggressive teens descended en masse from *les banlieues*, the suburbs, by way of the RER station buried below. "I know you want pictures, but save your memory space, trust me," I told her. And then, ten minutes later, "See what I mean? That's your money shot."

We had reached the Seine, and I pointed across the city to where the iron latticework of the Eiffel Tower shot up eighty-one stories over the Parisian rooftops. It was cheesy, but seeing that pointy silhouette never failed to make my heart flutter. I was happy to see it had the same effect on Mom and Bob.

After a flurry of photos, we continued our tour. We went to the *marché aux fleurs* on the Île de la Cité, the geographical center of the city, and ogled the lavender plants, bouquets of ranunculus, and petite olive trees in terra-cotta planters. We passed the green bookstalls along the Seine's banks and the rows of souvenir boutiques pawning identical magnets, aprons, T-shirts, and shot glasses. Outside Notre Dame, we craned our necks to see the famed gargoyles and admire the sculpted Gothic portals while the deeply moving bells clanged at noon. We strolled along rue Saint-Louis-en-l'Île on the Île Saint-Louis, peeping in the shop windows where everything from ash-dusted, pyramid-shaped goat cheese to folded silk scarves were displayed as expertly as curated art exhibitions. It was a thrill to lead them around the city, watching them rendered speechless by so much beauty. And after all the time I had been devoting to becoming a proper local, it was fun for me to play tourist.

We crossed to the Left Bank, past the Sorbonne and the giant bookstores and camping outlets. We stopped at a little café and ordered a lunch of salads, omelets, and roast chicken from the chalkboard menu. And, after slowly strolling through Saint-Germain's pedestrian-packed streets, admiring the chic Frenchies who were, in turn, admiring the *vitrines* of Yves Saint Laurent, Sonia Rykiel, and L'Artisan Parfumeur, we arrived at the Jardin du Luxembourg, where the magnolia, dogwood, and lilac trees were in full bloom. The sprawling lawns glowed green, their spring debut especially vivid. Impossibly cute kids rode donkeys, and serious old men tossed metal balls—*pétanque*, I explained to Mom and Bob—a sort of lawn bowling favored by old-timers.

By then, it was getting late. We had logged several miles with nary a peep of achy knees or blistered feet from either Mom or Bob. Did they want to Métro back, I asked preemptively. *Mais non!* They wanted to see more. I was beginning to see that they were falling in love with Paris.

So we dawdled at another picture-perfect café with *trois crèmes*, the closest thing to giant American coffees with milk, normally reserved for breakfast only, but we needed to reinforce ourselves for the return home, and I wasn't going to let French protocol slow us down now, not on that glorious day. Fortified, we crossed back over the Seine, taking the pedestrian bridge, Le Pont des Arts, for its charm and views. *There's the Eiffel Tower again*, I showed them. *And that massive building there? That's the Louvre!* Mom and Bob spun themselves around, taking it all in with starry eyes. *And look, right there, that's the tip of Île de la Cité, where we were earlier today. And just look at that perfect singular weeping willow at the tip of the island.* I joined their reveries. That lone tree always slayed me.

In just seven hours, Mom and Bob had seen many of Paris's classic landmarks. I knew it had been a great day. But still, it wasn't until dinner that I knew how deeply they were affected.

———— ✸ ————

We were all pretty tired when we got back to the tree house and decided to make sandwiches for dinner rather than go to a restaurant. So Mom and I left Bob in care of Milo and wended our way back down those six flights of stairs to pick up goods for dinner.

I loved shopping on rue Montorgueil so much that I often carted home more food—slices of spinach and goat cheese *tourtes*; jars of lavender honey and cherry jam, tiny, wild handpicked strawberries; *fraises aux bois*—than one person alone could possibly eat. Now at least I had an excuse to fill up my canvas shopping bag.

"Doesn't it smell amazing?" I gushed once we had crossed the threshold of my favorite *boulangerie*. Mom, standing inside the doorway clutching her purse, just nodded as she filled her lungs with the warm, yeasty air, her eyes alight with a brightness I didn't remember from home. With a fresh-from-the-oven baguette in hand, we went to the Italian *épicerie*, where from the long display of red peppers glistening in olive oil, fresh raviolis dusted in flour, and piles and piles of *salumi*, *soppressata*, and *saucisson*, we chose some thinly sliced *jambon blanc* and a mound of creamy mozzarella. At the artisanal bakery, Eric Kayser, we took our time selecting three different cakes from the rows of lemon tarts, chocolate éclairs, and what I was beginning to recognize as the French classics: dazzling *gâteaux* with names like the Saint-Honoré, Paris-Brest, and Opéra. *Voilà*, just like that, we had dinner and dessert. We headed back to the tree house—those pesky six flights were *still there*—and prepared for our modest dinner *chez-moi*.

Mom set the table with the chipped white dinner plates and pressed linen napkins. I set out the condiments—Maille Dijon mustard, tart and grainy with multicolored seeds; organic mayo from my local "bio" market; and Nicolas Alziari olive oil in a beautiful blue and yellow tin—and watched them get to it. They sliced open the baguette, the intersection of crisp and chewy, and dressed it with slivers of ham and dollops of mustard. I made a fresh mozzarella sandwich, drizzling it with olive oil and dusting it with salt and pepper. Moments later, we sat down and bit in.

"Oh my God!" Bob exclaimed. There was a pause while we waited for him to finish chewing. "Why can't Americans make bread like this? Those things they call 'French baguettes' at home?" He examined his sandwich in disbelief. "Those aren't baguettes! They're nothing like this!" He took another bite. My own sandwich was crusty and crunchy on the outside, pinchably soft on the inside. "My god, I don't think I've ever tasted anything like this. This is incredible." Mom nodded in agreement, but in barely two minutes, she had stealthily put away half her sandwich. The more we ate, the slower Mom and Bob went, as if prolonging the taste of simple perfection.

Then we moved onto our favorite course, dessert. As I sliced the small *gâteaux* we had selected at Eric Kayser into thirds, each of us did a little dance of excitement in our seats. The first two square tarts, pistachio-raspberry and pear-grapefruit, were both built upon thick, moist shortbread crusts, the only difference between them being the beautiful marzipan center of the pistachio-raspberry slice. The third cake was a dreamy dark chocolate creation that included layers of praline, mousse, and ganache. Mom took a bite of the pistachio-raspberry cake and put down her fork. It was almost as if she were disgusted, but it was just the opposite.

"Now that," she declared, "is delicious." The tone of her voice exposed barely concealed contempt for all the previous desserts we had ever eaten together in America. All the chocolate cakes, apple pies, and raspberry streusels—at that moment, they were all poor imitations of what dessert was supposed to be like. I started giggling at Mom's reaction, and Bob followed. Then, in all seriousness, we turned back to dessert. There was more stunned silence, more looks of disbelief. More food heaven. This, I was discovering, was one of my favorite things about Paris.

—— ✳ ——

For the next several days, Mom and Bob were total troopers. We hauled ourselves from Saint-Germain to the Marais, from the Bastille to Montmartre. We climbed the Eiffel Tower and walked the Champs-Élysées. From the monumental church, La Madeleine, in the eighth arrondissement, we walked east to the quiet charm of the Palais-Royal's gardens. We sampled morning pastries at Stohrer, afternoon *gâteaux* at Ladurée, and anything that struck our fancy at the countless neighborhood *boulangeries* we passed. On the very last day of their visit, we were faced with what every traveler dreads: rain. There was only one thing to do, and that was go to the Louvre.

What can I say about the Louvre? To date, I had logged about eight months of my life in Paris and made it to the world's most visited art museum exactly once: on a drunken midnight run with my college friends when we illicitly frolicked in the fountains surrounding I. M. Pei's glass pyramid. This visit with Mom and Bob was slightly more dignified.

All three of us were prepared to be impressed, but even so, we underestimated the museum's magnificence. Its size and scope were incomprehensible, with frescoed ceilings floating about one hundred feet over our heads and never-ending corridors and wings that extended forever before linking to more corridors and wings. And then there was the art: canvases the size of Alabama trailer homes and sculptures of every god and mortal throughout history. There were French Rococo and Italian Renaissance paintings, ancient Greek sculptures and Egyptian decorative art, Dutch Baroque and early Netherlandish, Islamic, Etruscan, Hellenic, Roman, Persian…There was the massive 1563 painting *The Wedding at Cana*, featuring a feast just a little bit larger and more ravishing than ours had been that week, and, of course, the *Mona Lisa*, which was swarmed by mobs of tourists aiming their digital cameras at her ambiguous smile.

But for me, there was nothing more stunning than the Winged Victory of Samothrace. As we approached the goddess Nike, rising step by step up the Daru staircase, her beauty loomed over us. The outstretched wings, the flowing garments, the forward movement—it was both graceful and powerful; there was so much emotion chiseled in that stone-cold marble. I kept turning around and around her, looking at her from the left, and then the right, and then from straight on. My heart was beating in overdrive, and my arms were covered in goose bumps. I'm not normally so moved by art, but that sculpture reduced me to mush. Feeling overwhelmed to the brink of exhaustion, Mom, Bob, and I decided it was time to do what we did best: break for sweets.

—— ✳ ——

Being that we were in the first arrondissement, given that it was a crappy day, knowing Mom and Bob as I know them, there was only one place for us to go: Angelina. This century-old tea salon, or *salon de thé,* on rue Rivoli is a classic tourist trap. But it's not without its charms. The Belle-Époque architect Édouard-Jean Niermans's interior still evokes elegance of decades past, when the likes of Coco Chanel and Audrey Hepburn—not schleps like us, in our sneakers and rain gear—stopped in for tea. It was founded in 1903 by the Austrian confectioner Antoine Rumpelmayer and named after his daughter-in-law. The whole atmosphere feels opulent, with gilded crown moldings, petite pedestal tables topped in marble, and pastoral landscapes reflected in arched mirrors hanging around the room, all bathed in a warm yellow glow. And then, of course, there is the world-famous *chocolat chaud.*

Can liquid be considered a proper dessert? *Oui,* in the rare instance that it's something as exquisite as Angelina's signature *chocolat "l'Africain."* So obscenely thick and outrageously rich, it's even better than when, as a kid, I'd sip Swiss Miss hot cocoa and savor those mini-marshmallows after sledding on an icy winter day.

Angelina's hot chocolate is so smooth and velvety, each sip sensually coats your tongue and teeth. It's both refined and indulgent; it's a simple recipe but a sophisticated experience. It arrives on a silver tray and is served perfectly warm—not scalding hot—with a side of whipped cream sculpted into a decorative puff. It's the perfect way to warm up on a rainy spring day. A decadent way to get your day's chocolate quota. It's hot chocolate worth the price of airfare to Paris.

"This reminds me of the cocoa from Jacques," my mom said, daintily blowing into her fine white cup.

Bob's face, flushed with the rich drink, broke into a grin. "Ohhhh, butt-her!" he cried in a pitch that pained my ears and made a nearby table of Harajuku girls look over at us in alarm. As soon as I made eye contact with them, they turned away and started giggling among themselves. Half the patrons in the airy tearoom were Japanese. The rest were a mix of Americans and Germans, with just a few French *grandes dames.*

"You can never have too much butt-heeeer!" He was doing his impression of Julia Child cooking with Jacques Pepin. The two masters had famously fun banter on their PBS series, *Julia and Jacques Cooking at Home,* and it never failed to make

Mom and Bob roll with laughter when they recalled, and imitated, the pair's strange and charming dynamics. They loved their cooking shows.

"Yeah, but I'm talking about the other Jacques," my mom said, rolling her eyes, despite her amusement.

"I knnnoooooow," Bob said, not giving up. A waitress, who still looked bedraggled in her formal black dress and white apron, briskly walked by and shot us a look of disapproval. But even I was having a hard time keeping a straight face. "But I like talking about...the...butt-heeeer!"

While Bob continued amusing himself with his ridiculous Julia Child impersonations, Mom and I started reminiscing about "the other" Jacques: Jacques Torres.

— ✳ —

We had made the pilgrimage to Jacques Torres's original boutique in the industrial Brooklyn neighborhood DUMBO years ago. Come to think of it, our adventures that week in Paris weren't much different than the ones we had shared in New York. We'd basically build an itinerary around a couple sweet spots that were on our radar—either destinations Mom had heard about on the Food Network or new bakeries I wanted to check out for my "Sweet Freak" column. Past explorations had brought us to Doughnut Plant on the Lower East Side for square yeast doughnuts glazed with peanut butter and filled with blackberry jam. We'd gone to Crumbs for those five-hundred-calorie, candy-covered cupcakes. And on the Upper West Side, we'd visited Alice's Tea Cup for the miraculously moist banana-butterscotch scones. But Mom and Bob were as big of chocoholics as I was, and the journey to Jacques Torres was memorable for more reason than one.

DUMBO, Down Under the Manhattan Bridge Overpass, wasn't the typical neighborhood I took them to. Ordinarily, we stayed within the comfy confines of New York's well-lit and scrubbed areas: Central Park, Soho, Grand Central. In Soho, the cobblestone streets are filled with moneyed European tourists. In DUMBO, they're littered with discarded vodka bottles and dog poop. Uptown, the limestone townhouses glow, spick-andspan. Here, a beautiful yet abandoned brick warehouse was splattered with graffiti and vomit. The subway rattled overhead, trains going to and fro on the Manhattan Bridge, and there was nary a soul about. Mom and Bob played it cool, but I think we all breathed a little easier once we entered Jacques's chocolate den.

Jacques is French and, at the age of twenty-six, was actually the youngest chef to win the prestigious Meilleur Ouvrier de France award, the highest honor possible in French pastry. He then came over to the United States, where he worked as a pastry chef at the Ritz in Rancho Mirage, California, and Atlanta, Georgia. Then he really made a name for himself as executive pastry chef of the highly acclaimed New York restaurant Le Cirque, which has also helped launch the careers of Daniel Boulud, David Bouley, Bill Telepan, and many others. Somewhere along the way, Jacques picked up the very American nickname Mr. Chocolate, and he finally realized his dream of opening his own chocolate business in 2000—the boutique where we found ourselves on that cold but sunny winter day.

After the barren landscape outside, it was like walking into a warm, welcoming womb—one that envelops you in the scent of chocolate and encourages you to go ahead, indulge! *Life is short. Eat dessert first!* Exposed brick walls and tin ceilings hinted at the space's earlier life as a warehouse, but its present incarnation was bright and modern. Shelves were jam-packed with orange and brown packaged treats: chocolate-covered Cheerios, chocolate-covered cornflakes, chocolate-covered raisins and pretzels and espresso beans. Chocolate malt balls, chocolate almonds, and giant 2.2-pound "Big Daddy" chocolate blocks. There was caramel corn, peanut brittle, mudslide cookie mixes, and tins of chocolate shavings so you could try replicating Jacques's über-rich hot chocolate at home—anything the choco-obsessed could dream was crammed in the small space.

An L-shaped counter had all manner of fresh, handcrafted temptations: a spread of individual bonbons with cheeky names like Wicked Fun (chocolate ganache with ancho and chipotle chilies), Love Bug (key lime ganache enveloped in white chocolate), and Ménage à Trois (a mystery blend of three ingredients). Platters of double chocolate chip cookies and fudgy brownies. And there were his buttery croissants and *pain au chocolat*, which duked it out in popularity with the French bakery across the street, Almondine.

But we had come for the cocoa, so we got in line—for despite the empty streets outside, plenty of tourists, many of them European, had also found their way from Manhattan's crowded streets to Mr. Chocolate. Bob managed to snag one of only two marble-topped café tables wedged in the tiny retail space, while Mom and I ordered three steamed cocoas and brought them to the table. The paper cups they were served in didn't do the rich drinks justice. The cocoa was worthy of France's finest porcelain cups and saucers. It was creamy, thick, and, *oui*, chocolaty. At the time, we agreed it was some of the best hot chocolate we'd ever tasted. Who knew that just a few years later, the three of us would be sipping incredibly decadent hot chocolate again, thousands of miles away in Paris?

———— ✸ ————

Warmed by Angelina's divine *chocolat chaud*, fatigued from the massive museum visit and days of touring Paris, we sat in contented silence. I replayed Mom and Bob's banter from throughout the week, which wasn't exactly as witty as Jacques and Julia's, but had its own sincerity and charm.

"I didn't know there were so many things you could do with puff pastry."

"I didn't know there were so many things you could do with whipped cream."

"I don't think I've ever taken a picture of my dessert before."

"I don't want this to end."

I knew it had been a successful visit. It wasn't just that Mom and Bob had been atop the Eiffel Tower at night or lit candles at Notre Dame. It wasn't just being able to finally say they'd visited the Louvre or eaten a real French baguette. It wasn't even the rich cocoa or moist, crumbly cakes or flaky *viennoiserie* that made them sigh in disbelief. Well, actually, maybe it was those things—if only a little bit.

But sitting in that historic tea salon, at once regal and relaxed, I knew they now understood my love for Paris and why I'd had to come back to it. Each sip and every bite we shared on their visit was an introduction to my new life. I was revealing a part of myself that I could never convey in words. It was bittersweet for all of us there at Angelina. They knew I intended to stay in Paris for a while. But while I may have moved thousands of miles away, at that moment, I felt closer to home than ever.

Whack rules in New York. Everyone has to be wild, outrageous, excessive— anything to be different from everyone else. And that includes our hot cocoa. Every February, for example, Maury Rubin hosts the Hot Chocolate Festival at City Bakery with a special flavor featured each day, from spicy fig to bourbon to tropical. I still haven't gotten through all the flavors but can wholeheartedly vouch for City Bakery's out-of-this-world classic cocoa, served year-round. Opt for the giant homemade marshmallow floating on top to sweeten things up even more. Another fancy favorite is the white hot chocolate with lemon myrtle and lavender at Vosges Haut-Chocolat in Soho.

I really do think Angelina's chocolat chaud *is the creamiest and dreamiest in Paris. But I also would never say no to a pitcher at Jacques Genin in the Marais or Les Deux Magots in Saint-Germain, both sinfully thick and delicious ways to get your choco-fix. For something approaching New York's adventures in fun flavors, head to the second-level tearoom of Jean-Paul Hévin for decadent raspberry-, matcha-, or ginger-flavored cocoa.*

CHAPTER 4

BONDING OVER FRENCH VIENNOISERIES

*A*fter Mom and Bob's visit, the social front picked up. The girls came and we shared four fabulous days and nights of eating our hearts out, pouring our souls out, and laughing our heads off. We luxuriated in the spring sunshine at the Jardin du Luxenbourg, toured the Seine from a boat at twilight, and sat in infinite cafés, comparing *café crèmes* and croissants, all the while catching each other up on our lives. And while I had fared pretty poorly on the restaurant front—not yet knowing the best spots or realizing that you absolutely must have reservations in Paris; walk-ins are rarely accepted—we'd managed at least one magical meal at Chez Janou, a Provençal bistro in the Marais.

After spending hours exploring the historic quartier, pausing only once from shopping to sit on the grass in the perfectly symmetrical park, Place de Vosges, we walked north and stumbled into this cute and colorful restaurant as the lunch rush was dying down. Sitting at a table in the back, we grinned at each other, finally experiencing that "ahh, yes, *this* is the meal we've been waiting for" feeling.

First came the rustic country bread with an almost tart sourdough flavor that was served with a bottle of freshly pressed olive oil and a small dish of pungent whole olives. We savored these southern beauties and sipped rosé while strategizing what to choose from the menu—from ratatouille to stuffed peppers to sea bass grilled with pesto, you could just imagine the bountiful flavors that lay ahead. I ended up ordering *brandade de morue*, a traditional dish from the south of France of salt cod pureed to the consistency of instant mashed potatoes and baked to rich, buttery perfection in a terrine—it was totally new to my taste buds and utterly delicious. We were all in love with our meals and didn't even save room for dessert, but, even so, there was something so decadent, and so perfect, about the five of us sitting there at four o'clock in the afternoon with full bellies and wine buzzes.

But the problem with having visitors, I discovered, was the deafening silence after they left. I had been in Paris for several months now and was accustomed to taking countless solo strolls, feeling pangs of envy as I walked by the cafés with their jam-packed terraces of cavorting friends and no way of breaking in. But when the girls returned to the States, the void they left was giant. Thankfully though, I was beginning to make new friends on this side of the Atlantic.

— ✹ —

Yummy...

...A hot handmade bread.

...A super flaky apple turnover fulled with real fruits.

...The surprising flavor of cumin in an olive bread.

Sounds good for you?

For someone who had studied French in high school and college, in groups and one-on-one, via cassettes and with workbooks, and yet never exceeded a third-grader's proficiency, I had grossly underestimated how long it would take me to pick up the language. Even Josephine's best efforts were taking eons to sink in.

But it had never even crossed my mind that it might also take forever to meet people. Unlike my pathetic linguistic skills, making friends had always been relatively easy for me. In addition to the girls from high school, I still have strong bonds with my college roommates and friends from San Francisco. At previous jobs, my team members and I were always chummy. Granted, it's somewhat a by-product of advertising—a young and boozy, glamorous and grueling industry where frequent happy hours and debauched bashes, interspersed with mad hours and the occasional all-nighter, provide the perfect bonding opportunities—but still, at every agency, I've walked away with at least one friend for life. Not so in Paris.

My colleagues at Ogilvy were a worldly and motley bunch. There was Pat, the Labrador-puppy-friendly Irish guy who sat next to me and always thought out loud and farted silently, and Lionel, my kilt-wearing, mohawk-shorn, French-Vietnamese art director partner who, despite his rock-and-roll looks, was so shy and soft-spoken, I felt as loud as a Texan in a ten-gallon whenever I spoke to him. My bobo ("bourgeois bohemian") creative director, Fred, who breezed in and out of the office for frequent scooter rides across town to meet the client and even more frequent smoke breaks, was cool. But he rarely had time to pause and ask *ça va?*, much less how this foreign city and life were treating me. There were a couple of old-timers who reeked of nicotine and coffee and muttered between themselves in the corner, and a group of scruffy hipster dudes who always looked like they'd spent the night on the couch. Everyone else pretty much blended into one big, buttoned up "colleague" group. They were all nice enough. But, so far, I wasn't clicking with any of them.

Until Isabelle. Another writer on the Louis Vuitton account, she and I started a friendship on a very auspicious note.

—— ✳ ——

I was sitting at my desk, the brilliant afternoon sunlight warming my back, trying to come up with a smart and clever title for the filmmaking competition we were launching for Louis Vuitton—anything but the after-school-special-ish "Destination: Inspiration" the client had suggested—when I saw a tall, thin girl with spiky blonde hair approaching. Isabelle had a free-spirited wardrobe—paisley bandanas, platform sandals, bracelets that clanked and echoed across the room—that matched her quirky beauty and brilliant smile. "Spunk" was the word that came to mind whenever we were in meetings together. She was Canadian, not French, which meant she wasn't too cool to express enthusiasm with a broad smile or wink of conspiracy. We had been making tentative steps toward friendship beyond our small Louis Vuitton team, and I knew I liked her for a reason beyond her laidback vibe.

"Bonjour, Amy," she spoke slowly, tentatively, hovering in the pool of sunlight. She placed a sheet of paper on my desk and pointed to the list of names with scribbled food items next to them. *Françoise, croissants; Veronique, jus de fruits; Gurvan, baguette.* She was organizing a *petit dej*—a potluck breakfast—for the creative department, she explained, pointing to the very official sign-up sheet. "Peut-être tu peux apporter du brioche, ou Nutella ou quelque-chose?" she asked, wondering what I could contribute. I wasn't exactly sure what this breakfast business was about; it seemed much more casual than I was accustomed to at the office. But my spirits perked right up at the thought of sweet, doughy breads and thick hazelnut spreads.

"Absolutement!" I said, already calculating that the deliciousness would begin in about, oh, eighteen or nineteen hours. "Bonne idée." I smiled at her before spelling out my name, pausing, and writing pain au chocolat next to it. "J'apporte combien, tu pense?" I asked in my embarrassingly primitive French. "Douze? Quinze?" Should I bring twelve or fifteen?

Her green eyes widened. "Non, non. Tout le monde apporte quelque-chose, donc, tu pourrais apporter juste cinq ou six. Il y aura beaucoup!" Duh. How un-French. My first instinct was to load up the table with an overabundance of food but she was telling me just five or six would do. Of course the Frenchies would be more restrained. But still, the American side of my brain rationalized, bringing only a half dozen pastries to my first office gathering? Didn't that seem sort of chintzy? I mentally noted to bring ten.

My demeanor must have changed as I was considering the vast quantities of pain au chocolat that were in my future.

"Tu aimes des viennoiserie?" Isabelle asked, with a knowing smile, if I liked pastry. This was my first dose of office small talk, I realized.

"Connais-tu des bons *boulangeries* à Paris?" And, if I

understood her correctly, I loved the topic of our conversation: pastries and bakeries.

Of course I had already mentally been going through my pâtisserie spreadsheet, thinking this breakfast would be the perfect occasion to try one of the *grandes classiques* like Lenôtre or Fauchon. What a way to make an impression, I thought, to bring some of the finest pastries in Paris. But there was also a small neighborhood *boulangerie* near the office whose rich, buttery smells emanating from the back door made my stomach rumble each morning. A modest but delicious score would be just as appreciated.

"Oui," I confessed. "J'adore ven-ny…vien-wah…ven-iseries," I stuttered. *Merde*, why did this beautiful and important word that encompassed the whole family of cottony soft breakfast pastries—classic croissants, *pain au chocolat, chausson aux pommes*—have to be so hard to wrap my tongue around?

"Vee-en-wah-sir-ie," Isabelle sounded it out, as patient and good-natured as a kindergarten teacher.

"Vien-y…ven-iseries," I tried again. We both laughed. Before moving on with her sign-up duties, Isabelle must have sensed that she had a hopeless sweet freak on her hands. She emailed me later that day, giving me a new address to add to my growing list of must-try Parisian *boulangeries*:

Here is some of my favorites addresses for a happy
sunday (or any other day!)

All is just per-fect at Du Pain et Des Idées

And if you don't already know Le parc de la Butte Chaumont, it's really nice, and pretty near of the bakery, so you can have a beautiful walk after a good bread time ;)

Have a good gourmet time!

...Sorry for my bad english!

Isa:)

Her email made my day. Already, I felt, she knew me well.

—— ✳ ——

From that afternoon on, Isabelle—Isa—and I were bona fide *amies*. After the *petit dej*, she organized picnics at Jardin de Luxembourg, with spreads of couscous salads, fluffed with exotic North African spices; sliced cantaloupe and sweet strawberries, speared on skewers; wheels of ripe Camembert and wedges of buttery Brie that were spackled on fresh, crunchy baguettes. She arranged visits to subterranean jazz clubs where natty couples twirled in the dark. And during office hours, we made a point of counseling each other in language—she wanting to practice English as much as I needed to keep learning French—resulting in classic Franglais conversations.

One day, I was trying to explain to her how excited I was to be in Paris—*excited* about my apartment, *excited* about my neighborhood, *excited* about my job and the city and traveling—when I learned an important lesson. "Je suis très excitant," I declared. She started laughing uncontrollably and then stopped abruptly, concerned that I might think she was laughing *at* me. "When you say, 'I'm excited,' it has very sexual connotations in French," she explained, searching for an alternative. "You can say, *j'ai hâte*," she enunciated the phrase as I blushed. "It means…I'm pressed."

"*J'ai hâte*," I repeated. Pressed, indeed, I was to stop making a fool of myself.

But Isa was one of the few people with whom I never felt embarrassed practicing—and, sadly, butchering—the language. For some reason, through my elementary French and her stunted English, we understood each other. We communicated with our eyes and our hearts. It was just one of those connections that felt easy and comfortable and natural—emotions that had been conspicuously absent since my family and friends had visited. I relished this budding new friendship. Each exchange, both tender and intrepid with our mishmash of cultural and language backgrounds, made me feel more connected, more normal. *Tu vois?* I said to Milo one perfect evening in the tree house after Isa had invited me to join her and a group of colleagues for lunch. *Making friends in Paris is a walk in le parc!*

— ✳ —

In June, Ogilvy threw a grand rooftop party for *fête de la musique*, a national holiday created for the sole purpose of celebrating music. It was an annual tradition for the agency to open its exquisite double-decker terrace high above the Champs-Élysées and hire DJs for the raucous holiday that falls on the summer solstice. It had been cloudy all day but the sun broke through around eight o'clock and people started filling up one terrace, and then the other. I psyched myself up to mingle with the agency VIPs, and I even managed to talk to the one cute colleague I had seen around the office.

I stumbled through French but defaulted to English, still surprised at how eager everyone was to practice their own foreign language skills. The French attitude to language had changed so dramatically since my college days in the '90s. Back then, most everyone all but refused to utter a word of English, even if they could. Now, they knew speaking English was essential to getting ahead in the workplace. Though some of them still resisted out of pride or self-consciousness, put a drink in them and their lips loosened right up.

The party had gorgeous cheese spreads, unlimited wine, fresh fruit, and, *hmmm*, hot dogs? I looked around for someone who might also think this was hilarious, but, in fact, everyone was devouring the American barbecue staples, ketchup, mustard, and all. It reminded me how half the workers on the Champs-Élysées toted bags from McDonalds or Quick every day at lunch. For all their panache, the Frenchies could be shockingly lowbrow.

As if the backdrop wasn't stunning enough—the Champs-Élysées buzzing below and the Vuitton flagship winking from across the street, the Grand Palais and Place de la Concorde down the boulevard, the Louvre and Notre Dame further off in the distance, and even Sacré-Coeur sitting placidly like dollops of *crème Chantilly* up on its hill in Montmartre— the Eiffel Tower did its strobe light spectacular on the hour, every hour. That night, there were also fireworks over Place de la Concorde to honor Charles de Gaulle's historic call to resist the Nazis back in 1940. I couldn't get over it. It was like a movie set, except it was my life, in Paris.

Finally, a fun party at work! I thought, watching everyone laugh and mingle, the red tips of their cigarettes like little party favors twinkling in the air as they gesticulated in lively conversations. The bottles of wine were disappearing and everyone was cutting loose. As the summer sky turned from pink to dusty purple to black, the rooftop became a pulsing dance floor.

I was in high spirits too. In addition to Isa, I had recently befriended an American expat with whom I instantly clicked, Melissa. She and I had been "set up" by my good friend from high school, Ben. When you move to a foreign city, all of your friends want to introduce you to their friends, friends of friends, or anyone they know who's remotely sane and English-speaking in the same city. Usually these friend-dates are train wrecks as you have nothing in common with the other person aside from both being sane Anglophones. Lucky for me, Ben knew better.

The first time Melissa and I got together, we poured our souls out to one another over Belgian beers on a café terrace. Not long after, we went slumming it to the Les Halles Cineplex to see Tom Hanks in *Angels & Demons*, a movie I would never have seen in New York but which brought me a strange sense of comfort and patriotism abroad. After that, I knew I had my partner in crime in all things cheesy, dorky, and American. Between Melissa and Isa, I felt like I had hit the friend jackpot in too-cool-for-school Paris.

Then Isa, who had been making the rounds (she was loved by everyone, not just me), gave me her news. "Tu connais Alexi et moi retournons à Canada?" she asked over the blaring techno, which was being spun by a guy I worked with on the Vuitton team on a daily basis. Rocking his head to the beat, headphones held up to one ear, I saw a totally different side to his cerebral explanations of a proper website user experience.

"Quoi?" I shouted back, thinking I hadn't heard her correctly. She couldn't be moving back to Canada—she was such an integral part to the Vuitton team and Ogilvy office. Her eyes were welling up with tears. *Had* I heard her correctly? If so, for better or worse, my French was really coming along.

Isa guided me over to the quieter edge of the terrace. "Oui. Nous partons." She went on to explain that she and her boyfriend were going to get married, and they wanted to be close to their families back in Québec. That as soon as Alexi was done with his baking apprenticeship, they were leaving Paris and returning to Canada. And that she had given notice to Ogilvy. I was stunned. My girl, my one fun female friend, was leaving. Say it wasn't so! But I felt even worse for Isa. Her tears began to spill over, down her cheeks, and I could viscerally feel her torment. "Il me manque déjà," she said, gesturing to the ridiculous 360-degree view of Paris we had. *She already missed it.*

It wasn't just the city's beauty, though, with the Eiffel Tower's lights dancing in the distance, of course that was a big part of it. But as we stood and talked about life and love and Paris, I understood her sadness and felt it as if it were my own. I realized how attached I was becoming to a lifestyle that ambled gracefully instead of blazing full steam ahead. To a city where every neighborhood had not two or three, but four, five, or six *boulangeries* to choose from. To a world that valued pleasure above everything else.

Would I one day, like Isa, be welling up at the thought of leaving? For that matter, would I ever be ready to leave Paris?

— ✸ —

My parents divorced when I was eight, and I left home at seventeen. After four years of college in Boston—including those five glorious months studying abroad in Paris—came my time in San Francisco, and then New York. All that's to say, the idea of home has changed a lot in my life. My real, honest-to-goodness roots will always be Connecticut. But I think it's important to feel at home wherever you are in the world.

Early that summer in Paris, when I Vélib'ed home from work each night, it made me happy to be pedaling along my little route from the Champs-Élysées in the eighth arrondisse-ment to the Montorgueil quartier in the city center. It made me happy to realize that I *had* a little route, one that I loved. Then again, zipping past Lanvin, Louboutin, Costes, and Colette on rue Saint-Honoré—what *wasn't* to love? I'd arrive in my neighborhood, absorbing the buoyant energy of the cafés and shops and people. I loved how jammed the café terraces were, everyone enjoying a beer or wine before return-ing *chez-eux* for a home-cooked dinner. With daylight last-ing forever, the sun hanging in the sky until well past 10:00 p.m., I'd have a few happy hours to myself to wander rue Montorgueil and watch the fabulous hipsters in their scarves and Wayfarers. Or I'd simply hang out in my tree house, writing about my infatuation with Paris or the day's lost-in-translation moments on my blog, which I'd started to keep in touch with family and friends back home.

I was happy that Paris was finally feeling like home. It was comforting and exciting, and both familiar and new. In a city that's a gold mine of clichés, I thought of a real gem: Paris was where my heart was.

——— ✳ ———

Christophe Vasseur, meilleur boulanger de Paris en 2008. Pas beaucoup de variété, mais de la grande qualité et des chaussons aux pommes faits avec des vraies pommes! irrrrrrrrrrrésistible!

With Isa's departure on the horizon, she suggested a special outing for our last date. Her fiancé was wrapping up an apprenticeship at Du Pain et Des Idées, one of the best *boulangeries* in the city. Did I want to go visit him and get a private tour of the kitchen? *Um, does a baby cry when you take away its candy?*

So late one afternoon, we arrived at the award-winning bakery, which is wedged on a corner in Paris's greatest bobo paradise, Canal Saint-Martin. Though it's hipsterville outside, the inside of the bakery is infused with old-time charm. Antique wooden furniture, copper cookware, and giant sacks of flour add a rustic dash to the original Beaux Arts painted glass ceilings and gilded mirrors. The woman at the counter, recognizing Isa, gestured to the kitchen door, giving us the okay to go back. I felt like a rock star bypassing the customers who curiously watched us, two fair-skinned *étrangères*, go behind the closed doors.

Her boyfriend, Alexi, welcomed us into the compact kitchen, where he was making the evening baguettes. He showed us how the raw dough was shaped and placed on giant slabs of rolling canvases. He explained how the ovens were stacked, with the hottest ones at floor level. This is where the bakery's signature bread, the *pain des amis*, a wonderfully nutty-crusty-chewy bread that is now served at Alain Ducasse's renowned Plaza Athénée restaurant, was baked. The traditional baguettes were assigned a couple drawers above.

When it was time, we watched him yank open the oven doors and drag the baguettes onto a contraption that looked like a cross between an ambulance stretcher and grocery store conveyer belt. Some of them were *bien cuit*, cooked crisp and golden. Others were *moins cuit*, a smidge undercooked and chewier. He deftly scooped them all into cylindrical wicker baskets, which were then delivered to the front, where the line of eager customers was growing longer, now that it was later in the day. *Funny being on this side*, I thought, remembering all the times I had been one of those salivating customers, waiting for the evening's bake to appear fresh and warm from the kitchen.

We snooped around a bit more, inhaling the fermenting bread dough and peeking at the tools and equipment. Then it was time to sample the goods. Isa and I left Alexi, fatigued with his eight-hour shift coming to a close, to finish his kitchen duties while we returned to the front to choose our snacks.

Christophe Vasseur, the charming young *boulanger* behind Du Pain et Des Idées, prides himself on doing a few things and doing them extremely well. No candy-colored *gâteaux* or theatrical chocolate sculptures for him. Just honest to goodness breads, hand-crafted *viennoiserie*, and a select few seasonal tarts.

Isa and I started with a *chausson aux pommes*. Whereas many *boulangeries* fill these apple turnovers with jam or compote, Du Pain et Des Idées uses actual slices of fresh apples, and there's no mistaking the difference. The tender but chunky fruit was sweet and tart with a bit of bite, delicious in the summer afternoon sun. We then tore into a mind-blowingly flaky croissant. There were so many paper-thin golden layers, it looked like a sculpture. It was more exquisite than any other croissant I had seen before—crispier too, leaving a mosaic of pastry flakes scattered in our laps and down around our feet. And, saving the best for last, we tucked into *l'escargot chocolat pistache*, another lovely puff pastry creation, this one spiraling outward in the shape of a snail, like *pain aux raisins*. Except these superfine layers were piped full of pistachio *crème pâtissière* and flecks of chocolate. Everything we had was fresh, delicious, perfect.

It was a bakery and an afternoon every bit as exceptional as Isa.

———— ✳ ————

Just as it takes time for friendships to develop properly, you can't rush a great croissant. It's a truism I will never be able to deny after experiencing Christophe Vasseur's pastries that day.

"Making croissants is 2 percent theory and 98 percent practice," he told me when I tracked him down for his baking insights after that beautiful experience with Isa. He was referring to the importance of using your own hands, practicing again and again, versus relying on courses and training. And he should know. Vasseur's own apprenticeship—which he started at the age of thirty after ditching a glamorous job in fashion sales—didn't amount to more than three months. He learned everything through his own passion and tenacity.

"Lots of people said, 'You're crazy. It will never work,'" Vasseur remembers of his early years, when he was toiling eighteen hours a day, six days a week. Nobody understood the dramatic change in his career path. But that didn't stop him. Being a baker was something he had wanted to do since he was a boy when, growing up in the French Alps, his three town bakers simultaneously inspired and tempted him with their creations. "It was always like going to a magician's shop—the way you could smell things even before opening the door. It's an environment of pure magic to me: using your hands to transform something so simple into something so good and beautiful."

So despite everyone's skepticism, he kept at it, pursuing his life dream. He searched for and found the perfect space: a bakery that had been around for 120 years. It had also seen three bakers go bankrupt in seven years. It wasn't exactly a good omen, but the space had soul, which was all Vasseur needed. Adopting the words of French novelist Marcel Pagnol as his mantra—*I'm gonna make a bread like none other has ever tasted before and, in this bread, I will put a lot of love and friendship*—he opened his *boulangerie* in 2002.

"I didn't do it for myself, but I did it to share with people," he explains. "Baking is more than bread, more than flour and water and yeast. It's the desire to be more human and go back to the simple things. To go back to roots."

Vasseur makes it all sound so simple. But can the artful blending, rolling, folding, and baking of his fine and flaky croissants be easy? Sublime, yes; simple, *mais non*.

Of those dreamy, buttery, million-layered *viennoiserie*, which have earned him legions of fans and awards from the renowned Gault et Millau and Michelin Guide, he credits his drive and that he's always been good with his hands. Of course the ingredients matter as much as the passion and technique that get poured into them. Vasseur insists on top-quality organic flour, butter, milk, and eggs whenever possible. Equally important is the time and care invested.

Whereas industrial croissants can be churned out in thirty minutes thanks to premade dough, Christophe invests thirty-four *hours*. This is because he makes his own dough from scratch and gives it time to rest and develop its aroma—or, in his words, to benefit from "the magic of fermentation." He then takes that lovely, fragrant handmade dough, layers it with butter, folds and rolls it again and again, making way for those many fine, buttery pastry layers. Then they're cut into triangles, folded into the distinctive crescent shapes, and baked for fourteen minutes. The croissants puff, they expand, they turn golden brown in the oven. And, finally, heaven is served.

———— ✳ ————

Of course I was familiar with croissants before moving to Paris. But like all Americans, the samples I had grown up on were farces: ridiculous, oversweetened commercial attempts at French finesse. To get a quality croissant, you had to really search and sample. Or have friends in the know.

At a previous advertising job in New York, my friend Mary waltzed into the agency one morning carrying two paper bags, butter weeping through the thin paper. She gathered us girls—we were a klatch of five who loyally boozed, lunched, and commiserated with each other—and revealed the otherworldly contents. Inside the first bag were five golden croissants, folding in on themselves from their warmth. The other bag held just as many precious *pain au chocolat*, also still a titch warm from the morning bake. We huddled on the couch for an impromptu breakfast and with every one of our first bites, there were waves of ecstasy. *Where did these come from?* we demanded. We flagged the token Parisian in our office, whom, of course, I had a crush on. He confirmed what we already knew to be true: these were exquisite croissants.

Probably the best in the city. We were buzzing with this delicious and unexpected discovery for the rest of the day.

From then on, we all took our turns periodically bringing in bags of croissants and *pain au chocolat* from Pâtisserie Claude, the source of the buttery beauties. Going to the wee West Village bakery was part of the experience. Instead of a charming café or fancy pâtisserie you might expect of a French bakery in New York's most picturesque neighborhood, it was a shabby tin can of a place. Linoleum floors, fluorescent lights, and a few framed photographs on the wall revealed nothing of the prowess in the kitchen. And instead of a charming French baker like, say, Christophe Vasseur, Claude was cantankerous. He was a burly Frenchman who had been running the bakery for decades. He couldn't be bothered with press and didn't have time for adulation. He baked. That was it. *Ça suffit.*

But we—and scores of other cultish worshippers in the city—were hooked, evaluating what made Claude's croissants so good. There was the crisp and flaky shell that shattered when you bit into it, leaving that telltale bib of giant crumbs on your front side. And then an inside filled with light, tender layers that were slightly stretchy, but never doughy or overly chewy—the by-product of overworking the dough, I learned later from Christophe. And, of course, there was the beautiful taste of butter. Not grossly greasy, but rich and decadent. As warm as a summer day.

———— ✳ ————

After sampling our *viennoiserie* at Du Pain et Des Idées, it was time to leave. It was time to say good-bye to Isa.

I gave a farewell hug to Alexi at the bakery's back door, and then Isa and I walked toward the Métro on the chaotic Place de la République, a giant, leafy square that has more hobos and rowdy teenagers than magnificent monuments and fountains like Place de la Concorde on the other side of town. As we strolled, old men on café terraces were agog at Isa's long legs, which she dared to bare in short shorts in the summer sun. Though she had been my first French friend, her brazenness in a land of conformity reminded me that Isa, too, was *une étrangère*. She had come to Paris to live her dream. And now she was leaving to embrace a new one.

We double-kissed good-bye—now a natural gesture to me—and then held each other in a tight hug, which made me ache again for my friends back home and the one I was losing now. I was happy for Isa and her new life chapter, just as I was excited for me to stay in Paris. But it was a bitter-sweet moment. As I watched her disappear into the Métro, I couldn't help but wonder: if I continued to follow this trail of flaky croissant crumbs, where would the path take me?

MORE
Sweet Spots
ON THE
MAP

While more and more French boulangeries *are relying on premade pastry
dough (sacré bleu!), rest assured, they're still pretty good.
In fact, most croissants in Paris are still ten times better
than anything you'll find anywhere else in the world
(I chalk it up to the French butter). Even Monoprix,
the giant grocery store chain, has decent croissants. But
don't waste your precious* viennoiserie *moments at
Monoprix. Go to Gérard Mulot (in the 3e and 6e) for
an über-buttery creation, Sadaharu Aoki (in the 5e,
6e, or 15e) for the exotic matcha flavor, or Eric Kayser
(all over town) for a classic* croissant au beurre.

*New York's croissant options are few and far between.
Thank goodness for the French bakeries. Treat yourself
to an authentic experience—and your own giant bib
of flaky croissant crumbs—with a visit to Ceci-Cela or
Balthazar in Soho, Café Deux Margot on the Upper
West Side, or take a jaunt over to DUMBO and breakfast at Almondine Bakery.*

— [C H A P T E R   5] —

THE BIG APPLE DOES MACARONS

*I*n the eight years I had lived in New York, it always thrilled me to return to the city. Whether I was training back from a weekend at my dad's in Connecticut or landing at JFK after three weeks of hiking and biking in New Zealand, I could never suppress my grin when I saw the jagged skyline, the halo of light emanating from the city, the sea of yellow taxis, or the mishmash of cultures and clothing swimming together in one crazy orgy. New York was under my skin. For years, it had been my true love. And then Paris came along.

After spending my junior semester abroad in Paris, the city had blossomed into this little fantasy of mine. Paris was the romantic counterpart to my gritty reality in New York. But I never thought it would happen to me. In my mind, Paris was the guy who's super good looking *and* nice *and* interesting *and* romantic *and* fun. You mean, that guy actually exists? And he's interested in *me*? Oh please, I don't buy it, not for a New York minute.

But after nearly six months in Paris, I knew it was a fact: Fantasies do come true. Despite my moments of uncertainty and pangs of loneliness, I was loving life in Paris. I was so smitten with the Gallic city's grand, plane-tree-lined boulevards and ever-so-slightly crooked side streets, its countless café terraces and the ritual of lingering on them with a single *café crème* or *coupe de champagne*. Every time I biked by a *boulangerie* in the morning and got a whiff of the butter baking into the folds of pastry dough and baguettes being pulled fresh from the oven, I was seduced all over again.

It was a no-brainer to stay in Paris. When my initial six-month *contrat à durée déterminée*, the kind of work contract issued for a finite amount of time, was up at the end of summer, I eagerly re-signed, this time for nine months. Nine more months of working on Louis Vuitton, nine more months of living in my tree house, nine more months of European travels and sweet explorations. Nine more months of…Paris. I was mad for the place—I wasn't going to nip my love affair in the bud. But that didn't mean I wasn't also excited to be going home to New York for a two-week visit. In fact, with my trip on the horizon, I smiled, remembering my old lover's charms: things like pizza and chocolate chip cookies, fashion magazines and reality TV, gyms and taxis on every corner, *my friends*.

New York, here I come!

—— ✳ ——

Almost immediately upon touching down at the chaotic JFK, the duality of my life hit me. It seemed, for the first time since moving to and falling for Manhattan, things were going to be different. With the lovely, soft *pain aux raisins* from Stohrer still in my belly from breakfast in Paris that morning, I was assaulted by the smells of foot-long hot dogs and ten-ounce Cinnabons inside the airport terminal. Outside, the shrill shriek of car horns made me yearn for the relatively soothing clang of church bells in Paris. And everywhere I looked: big bottoms! Ginormous bellies! When did everyone get so fat?

On the subway ride into the city, I wrinkled my nose at the trashy tabloid magazines, at everyone shouting into their cell phones and snapping their gum, at the filth and graffiti covering the seats. Then I caught a glimpse of my puss reflected in the window, the city skyline visible in the distance, and I told myself to stop being such a snob. I was a New Yorker after all. *This* was my home; Paris was only temporary. Who was I to suddenly look down my nose at everything I had always regarded with such adoration?

—— ✳ ——

The first few days of the visit didn't get much better. It was taking me awhile to come out of my shell shock and fall back into a New York groove. It didn't help that AJ, my rock, was on a business trip in Dubai and I still hadn't seen her, or met this guy, Mitchell, with whom she had quickly become serious. I was keen to get to know who had stolen my best friend's heart but had to wait a couple more days for her return. In the meantime, what I needed was some good old American bonding. I rallied the troops at one of my favorite old haunts, Sweet & Vicious.

Everyone had been complaining about what a washout the New York summer had been, but after a perfect season in Paris I was now lucking out with a heat wave. It was a warm and still evening. The first to arrive, I settled on a picnic table bench on the bar's back patio with a fresh vodka tonic, admiring the brick tenement buildings looming over me with their rickety fire escapes—so New York! I was wearing a sleeveless grey silk blouse I had bought in one of the Marais's chic boutiques and sandals to show off my pedicure—the first one I'd had in six months, as they cost twice as much in Paris, and I stubbornly refused to spend €30 on having my toes polished when that money would be better spent on wine, cheese, and chocolate. Waiting on the patio, I had butterflies in my stomach as if an old flame was about to show up. It was the most excited I had been since arriving in New York.

"Amy, darlin'!" My six-foot-five-inch giant of a friend,

Jonathan, ducked through the door and enveloped me in a bear hug. "Oh, my girl. I'm so happy to see you." He looked down at me with his sideways smile and shook his head. *This is what I needed*, I told myself, melting into his mass, familiar and warm.

"You too, love! How are you?" I asked, buried in his armpit, which was both disgusting and wonderful. But I didn't give him time to answer. "Tell me what's going on at work," I commanded, reluctantly pulling away to look at his face. As a project manager, he was forever plotting to take over the production department of his ad agency. I knew that he had six months of intrigue and cattiness to unload and that other friends would soon arrive and interrupt us. He rolled his eyes and opened his mouth to share the latest drama when—too late—the girls arrived.

"Ammmmyyyy!" Melanie, Mary, Krista, and Carrie sprang through the back door, looking fabulous in their heels, handbags, and jewelry—New York to the nines. After sipping sidecars and sharing secrets for so many years, we were now like teenage girls reunited after the long summer vacation. Our chorus of squeals and hugs provoked a couple curious looks but everyone on the patio quickly turned back to their cocktails and conversation. A flood of happiness washed over me. It wasn't just seeing my friends again. But for the first time in months, I was at a normal bar where you stood around and socialized, instead of clustering yourselves in private groups around café tables. You could actually mingle and act rowdy—absolutely unacceptable behavior in Paris. Tonight, there was none of that impossibly hip and aloof French attitude. None of the cliquish there's-no-way-in-hell-you're-breaking-in-here protectionism. I was on familiar territory, in the arms of old friends. I had forgotten what the home court advantage felt like.

Within the hour, Mike and Corey showed up. Then Ben and Merrill. And Kurt and Christy. It had been a long time since everyone had been together and there was lots of catching up to do. As I looked around at my friends, I realized that while I had been settling into Paris, everyone here had been settling into domesticated bliss. Aside from my band of girlfriends from work, all my New York friends were paired up. It gave me a strange flashback to when I was six years old and would watch my parents' hippie friends with their cigarettes and joints, whiskey and rosé, mingling and laughing at casual parties on our big front porch. They had seemed so artsy and fabulous—so adult. I now found myself looking at my friends with the same wide-eyed wonder, and even a little bit of that little-girl envy. It was a strange pool of emotions that I suppressed by ordering another drink.

Hours later, the powder blue twilight had turned to night and I had downgraded from vodka tonics to beer. All the couples had returned to their apartments to walk their dogs—clearly in training for the next step: babies. It was just the tribe of us single girls now. And as much as I loved my girls, I hated that New York was overrun by a million little groups just like us. It was inescapable: there were too many single ladies in this city.

The talk naturally turned to advertising since we had all met at the same agency years ago and bonded over office politics (and those incredible Pâtisserie Claude croissants). Stories started flying about who was working where and which senior VPs were acting naughty. The salaciousness of the business and dishing about it had always been a guilty pleasure of mine. But as Krista let loose on her old boss who had had not one, but two, interoffice affairs, as well as a second child with his wife in the past year, I couldn't rouse the proper disgust or delight. I dug for it, but—nothing. "The guy clearly has to go to sex addicts anonymous. It's like he's David Duchovny or something." Everyone else laughed at the reference to the Hollywood star's rehab stint for sex addiction, but I had started going numb.

I didn't know if it was the flood of emotions from seeing so many friends at once or if it was something else, but I suddenly didn't feel like myself. I was nodding my head at all the right points in the conversation, but inside I was floating away. I couldn't get close to anyone. These were friends who knew me inside and out. But they didn't feel the same. The bar and city didn't feel the same. *I* didn't feel the same.

"Have you been to the Standard Grill yet?" Mary asked.

She must have seen my eyes going vacant and was trying to steer the conversation into firm Amy territory. When I had lived in New York—*had it really been only six months ago?*—I wrote restaurant reviews and roundups for the local pubs, and religiously read every magazine and blog about food, restaurants, and the local dining scene. The girls always turned to me for the best first date, brunch, neighborhood gem, old-school New York, cheap Mexican, cool design, best bathroom, of-the-moment restaurant recommendations. "It just opened in the Meatpacking," Mary continued, trying to reignite my enthusiasm.

"Oh yeah, I heard that place is cool. The bar has ping-pong tables, right?" Melanie asked. Six months ago, ping-pong tables would have seemed novel. But ping-pong tables? Big whoop! They were de rigueur across Paris. I wasn't taking the bait, even when Carrie chimed in that she had gone to the hot spot last weekend and been within spitting distance of Bruce Willis, who was followed two minutes later by Demi and Ashton, plus a pair of lumbering six-foot, three-hundred-pound bodyguards.

This was the way things were now, I realized. For the past six months, my friends had been the ones scoping out and sizing up the newest, latest, coolest openings in Manhattan. They had been cruising right along without my tips and assessments, living in "my" city while I had been thirty-six hundred miles away. Things change every weekend in New

York. Restaurants open and close. Bars go from "It" to "Over It." Did I really expect that I could be gone for months and have everything remain the same? I was now a stranger in my hometown.

"Guys, I have to go," I said, putting my barely touched Stella on the table, debate over the most impossible dinner reservations hanging in the air. Everyone looked at me incredulously.

"What? You're leaving? Why? Let's go to Café Select for dinner!" Mary said. Meanwhile, Carrie's face was lit up from her BlackBerry. She was already shifting to Plan B.

"You know, I'd love to, but a massive wave of jet lag just washed over me," I begged. "I think I'd fall asleep in my spaetzle if I stayed out." It was true that I was still a bit woozy from jet lag. But I knew I'd return to my apartment for another sleepless night, no matter how tired I was. More than anything, I just didn't want to feel alienated any more. Everything I had once known and loved suddenly felt so foreign and I no longer knew where I belonged. This night that I had been deliciously anticipating had taken it out of me. I needed it to end.

—— ✳ ——

Walking around the neon-filled avenues and crowded streets in the ensuing days, I found myself having a mini identity crisis. So many of my friends, including AJ—who was back from her business trip and on for dinner that night—were moving in with boyfriends, and moving out to Brooklyn. Out of my entire community of New York friends, only a handful were still in the same place as me: single and living the life of a twentysomething. Cohabitation in Park Slope or Carroll Gardens was apparently the modern fairy tale of my peers, not whooping it up in a foreign country. I kept pondering where all these observations left me: with two homes, or none? Was I a New Yorker or a Parisian? Expat or local? Where exactly did I belong? As I searched for the connection to and love for a city that had always sustained me, I felt sad and alienated.

I also felt guilty on a more existential level. It was like realizing that you've fallen out of love with someone. Each morning, I'd wake up, hoping to feel differently, thinking but, but, but…I used to love this place. I used to look forward to this. This used to be my *life*. Now I felt bad because I couldn't get excited about something that I once loved so much. I couldn't help but see New York as loud and filthy instead of elegant and transporting. The tarted-up *Sex and the City* wannabes tottering in high heels and shockingly short skirts had none of the grace of French women who walked with a confident, sophisticated gait. The urban grit and tension felt claustrophobic, not inspiring the way Paris's cobblestone streets and plazas did.

It didn't help that as soon as I'd start feeling a New York

connection again, I'd be ushered back to Paris. For just as the French were having a love affair with cupcakes, I discovered New Yorkers were falling for the macaron.

———— ✻ ————

Ah yes, macarons. Those crisp but chewy, light-as-air meringue cookies. Not the big, hulking lumpish Italian confections that are often made with coconut. French macarons are different. They're delicate yet persnickety. A feat of mixing, folding, stirring, and timing. A delightful combination of powdered sugar, finely ground almonds, and egg whites and not much else, save for the luxuriously creamy ganache or buttercream filling that holds the two cookies together. Firm but tender, shiny yet ridged, with ethereally light shells and heavy middles, they're miniature studies of contrasts—and deliciousness.

Making macarons is famously difficult. Everything must be done just so: the ingredients measured to the very gram, egg whites aged and beaten on a rigid timetable, ovens heated to the precise degree—even the outside weather conditions can result in flat or cracked shells, instead of the shiny, perfectly domed specimens that beckon from pâtisserie *vitrines* and tea house cake stands. "Humidity is the enemy of macarons," is how the instructor explained it in a macaron-making class I took. (You better believe I took a macaron-making class. I figured with those things being as iconic to the Frenchies as cupcakes were to Americans, the least I could do was see what all the fuss was about. I spent a few hours on a Saturday, learning at La Cuisine Paris.)

If you don't stir the batter enough, you get spiky cookies. If you stir too much, they risk becoming flat. And anyone who's ever admired the lovely little things knows the cookie shells should be nice and smooth with a *jolie* sheen, while the inner lip, *le croute*, should be ragged. The innards should be moist, but not wet; the outside crisp, but not tough. The more you know about them, the easier it is to understand why macarons cost a couple bucks each.

When I arrived in Paris, I was ignorant to all this. My first clue to Parisians' devotion to the wee delights was when I coasted by Pierre Hermé's rue Bonaparte boutique on a Vélib' and saw a line snaking out the door. My curiosity was piqued but I had other, more decadent, sweets to sample. Like Jacques Genin's bittersweet chocolate éclairs and *Boulangerie* Julien's dense and creamy almond croissants. Later, it's true, I became a devotee of Pierre Hermé's cakes. But two-bite, pastel-colored cookie sandwiches seemed like child's play.

Then Lionel, my partner at work and a sweet freak himself, brought *une boîte de macarons* into the office. He visited my desk and deftly removed the lid, presenting an array of perfectly formed, vibrantly colored macarons. I was dazzled. The three perfect rows seemed almost too pretty to disturb. But then I realized that was nonsense. *Vite!* They should be sampled. It was time to lose my macaron virginity.

My fingers danced above the open box as I tried to antici-
pate which flavor would be the very best. Lionel, equal parts
benevolent and impatient, steered me to a dusty rose-colored
one; it was the famous Ispahan flavor. I bit into the shell
that, *poof*, crunched ever so delicately before collapsing in a
delightfully chewy and moist mouthful. And then the storm
of flavors hit me. Bright raspberry, exotic lychee, and a whiff
of rose. There was so much power in that pretty little thing.
It was a delicacy packed with skill, imagination, poetry, and,
God, give me another one!

As I drifted away on a little cloud of rose-tinted heaven,
Lionel decided to school me in a very important French lesson.

---- ✸ ----

In Paris, there are two kinds of people: those who think
Pierre Hermé makes the best macarons and those who
believe Ladurée's are the best. What many people don't know,
even ardent macaron worshippers, is that Pierre Hermé once
worked for Ladurée, the traditional *salon de thé* with roots
back to 1862.

One hundred and fifty years ago, Ladurée was just a bakery.
But as Paris's dramatic tree-lined boulevards and sweeping
gardens were being installed as part of Baron Haussmann's
nineteenth-century modernization program and café culture was coming full swing, Jeanne Souchard, Louis Ernest
Ladurée's wife, decided that ladies needed a place for social

outings. He merged the café concept with the pastry shop, *et voilà*, one of the first *salons de thé* was born. Though today it's a multimillion dollar empire, with locations in far-flung Japan, Turkey, and Saudi Arabia, Ladurée still retains the class and charm of the early days. The three Parisian tea salons share the same powder-green color scheme, Belle Époque interiors, and attract a mélange of Japanese tourists and ladies who lunch. It's iconic to some, stuffy to others. I think it's just lovely.

After an apprenticeship at Lenôtre and a ten-year stint at Fauchon, two other historic French pâtisseries, Pierre Hermé became consulting pastry chef at Ladurée, opening the magnificent Champs-Élysées location—the one, conveniently, right near Ogilvy. But ultimately, he was a little too rock and roll for the traditional outfit. The mix of fruity flavors that is Ispahan is the perfect example of why the pâtissier, Pierre Hermé, and the salon de thé, Ladurée, didn't mix. The flavor wasn't considered a success at Ladurée, so he took the recipe with him when he set out on his own in 1998.

Now Ispahan is his most celebrated flavor combination, but by no means the only one. Over the years he's created macarons such as chocolate and passion fruit; raspberry and wasabi; peach, apricot, and saffron; white truffle and hazelnut; and olive oil and vanilla. They may sound funky, but trust me, they are all delicious. And while Hermé also does classic, singular flavors—vanilla, pistachio, lemon, and rose, to name a delicious few—many would say that is where Ladurée rules.

If you ask me, both Pierre Hermé and Ladurée have their merits. Pierre Hermé's macarons are still made by hand; Ladurée's are assembled by machine. But Ladurée's macarons and boxes are also less expensive and the experience is more transcending. Brand and taste, preference and prejudices, the debate rages on: whose macarons are the perfect balance of crisp to chewy to melty? Who has the most sublime flavor combinations? Who has the richest ganache? Whose are the prettiest? Ultimately, it's a question that's nearly impossible to answer. Just exactly who has the best macaron: Pierre Hermé or Ladurée?

With my initiation to the city's great macaron rivalry under way, I started appreciating the delicacies for what they were: pretty and petite, feminine and elegant, fancy enough for *une soirée* but also indulged in as an everyday *goûter*. In other words, they were *totally* French. What were they doing all over New York?

— ✷ —

Back in Paris, Anglo-American restaurants and bakeries were springing up all over, studiously re-creating cheesecake, carrot cake, and, *bien sûr*, *le cupcake*. But when I saw the transatlantic love reciprocated, I just rolled my eyes. Seeing macarons in Manhattan was like going to Vegas and seeing the Eiffel Tower. It just felt so wrong. But I was finally knocked off my high horse when I happened by Kee's in Soho.

Kee Ling Tong was one of my favorite chocolatiers in New York. Years earlier, I had a fleeting addiction to her otherworldly *crème brûlée* truffle, a dainty yet dangerous homemade bonbon that you have to pop into your mouth whole, or suffer the consequences of squirting eggy custard all over your blouse. Now, I discovered, she was handcrafting macarons in wild and wonderful flavors like blood orange, sesame, and rose. How did she create her recipes? What inspired her expanded repertoire? And how did hers compare to Paris's best?

Emboldened as I was by my new French history lessons, I asked Kee in her Soho boutique: why macarons?

"Because they're so pretty!" Kee laughed. "They're so dainty. I think it's the colors." And, standing as we were above the glass display case, I had to agree. Her blueberry macarons were as bright as the September sky. The lotus flower was the kind of soft pink that's the perfect shade of blush. Kee's favorite flavor, passion fruit, was a snappy corn husk yellow. These were surrounded by greens (lulo and jasmine green tea) and purples (lavender, which was dotted with purple sugar crystals) and some neutral shades as well (white truffle oil and mint mocha).

"Yeah, I guess you're right. It's like an edible rainbow." As I was admiring the colors, Kee slid two of the jasmine green tea macarons across the counter, one to me and one for another customer, who had entered the closet-sized boutique with a big bouquet of helium balloons. "Oh, thanks!"

I said, delighted for the nibble. "Aren't you going to have one?" I joked.

"I don't like sweets," Kee responded.

"You don't like sweets?" I stared. "How can that be?"

She shook her head, gesturing to the two displays, the one filled with the pretty macarons and another case that had over a dozen varieties of dark chocolate bonbons. "I don't eat any of the chocolates or macarons—I only try them when I'm creating new flavors and need to taste them."

"Wow, that's incredible." I pondered this while crunching into the semi-chewy shell of the macaron. The ganache in the cookie's middle was less generous than those made in Paris but the balance between herbal and floral flavors was nice. "I'm jealous. If I didn't eat sweets, I'd be ten pounds lighter."

The other customer, a young Chinese guy, was listening to all of this with a small smile. "Do you come here a lot?" he asked me curiously.

"I've been coming here since—when did you open, Kee? In, like, 2003?"

Kee looked up at the ceiling, doing the math in her mind. "2002. June of 2002."

"Yeah, because I was working near here then. I remember my boss coming back from lunch one day and insisting I come here. He said it was the best chocolate he'd had in New York." I was answering the young man as much as letting Kee know that she had long-running loyalty in town. I loved that she had ditched her career in finance—which she began with a JP Morgan internship at the age of sixteen—when she realized "it wasn't fun anymore." It takes a strong woman to survive fifteen years in the finance industry, but a brave one to leave it. I would support her if she was pedaling bubble gum on the corner of West Broadway and Houston.

"What's your favorite chocolate?" he asked me.

"That's a good question." I stepped over to the case he was perusing. "Well, I'm a sucker for praline, so I don't think you can go wrong there, with the hazelnut praline," I pointed. I couldn't help but admire the beautiful sheen that all of her chocolates had; Kee was a master at tempering. "Mmmmm, otherwise, I'd stick to the fruit flavors since Kee loves fruit: kaffir lime, passion fruit, pineapple-lychee," I pointed to each. "The flavors just pop in your mouth." I was suddenly a budding salesgirl.

Before the customer had come in, Kee and I had been talking about her technique for creating fresh fruit purees for her macarons' ganache fillings. She was constantly experimenting with new flavors and added to the repertoire every couple of months. She had started with five and was up to twenty-two flavors, which she rotated, offering eight to twelve at any particular time. "People are adventurous—they want to try something different," she explained, which was why she focused on pairings instead of individual flavors. But

I didn't have the heart to tell her that ginger-peach was a far cry in adventurous eating from the fig and foie gras macaron that Pierre Hermé offered. I didn't want to squelch her devotion to the French treats in any way, and I was also trying to keep my "Parisian pride" in check.

Kee slid the box of chocolates, wrapped in rattan, to the young man. "Your friend is going to love the chocolates," I told him, suddenly feeling my loyalty to Kee extending in a fierce wave to all of New York. "It's a birthday gift, right?" I asked, looking up at the balloons. He nodded. "Yeah, trust me. They're New York's finest."

———— ✳ ————

I had double- and triple-checked that AJ's flight had landed and was looking forward to our dinner that night. As the day wore on, I was admittedly still wrapping my head around the fact that it would be a party of three.

"Bonjour!" A beaming man stepped forward to hug me hello when I entered Pó, the Carroll Gardens restaurant AJ had chosen for that night. I stole a quick look at his warm green eyes and hugged him back, already feeling a connection. Mitchell had lived in Paris for five years, and it was immediately clear our shared love for the city, not to mention AJ, was going to be the centerpiece of our bonding. I instantly relaxed and felt grateful for the sweet welcome.

Then I turned to AJ, who had chopped her blond hair into

a bob and was waiting for her turn to greet me. "Bonjour, Madame!" she sang out, the same way we often greeted each other since Madame Snitkin's French class, freshman year of high school. We kissed on both cheeks and rocked back and forth, hugging. It was a slightly surreal scene—greeting my best friend at an Italian restaurant in Brooklyn, after I had been in Paris and she in Dubai—but it was also strangely appropriate. Every time I was with AJ, I realized, everything felt normal.

The three of us were soon settled at our table with a bottle of celebratory prosecco, launching into hours of conversation. We lingered over creamy white bean dip, fresh tomato bruschetta, homemade gnocchi, and tuna seared to perfection—something the French, with all of their culinary prowess, hadn't quite mastered. It was all so delicious: the company, the conversation, and the food. Most important, though, I was relieved. I liked this guy, Mitchell.

"It's going to happen to you, Aim," AJ said earnestly when just the two of us were sitting outside, sharing latte macchiatos the next day in Nolita. As her best friend, it was obligatory that I give her new boyfriend a glowing review, which I could thankfully do in good faith. Mitchell was a great guy, and AJ was seriously happy. "I mean, it really does happen when you least expect it."

Ugh—and there it was: that tired expression dished to every single girl in America, ad nauseam. And AJ put it out there. I knew it was her job to pump me up, but why did my partner in crime have to use this cliché? The older I got, the more people said it to me. And at thirty-six, I was hearing it way too often. I swallowed a wave of irritation, determined to focus on the moment, on the positive. Here we were, after twenty-five years of dating hijinks, broken hearts, secret crushes, passionate flings, conflicted feelings, and unrequited loves, both in love-filled places: she with Mitchell, me with Paris.

"Oh, I know. It will happen." I paused, letting my defensive, knee-jerk response soften a little with AJ. "At least I *think* it will."

"It *will*, Amy," she responded emphatically. "Of course it will. It's all about timing."

"I know, I know," I trailed off, pondering my romantic past. From my first love in high school, I had gone straight into a four-year relationship at college. When school and the affair ended, I moved to San Francisco, and it was barely a year before I met and started dating Max. And when he and I finally parted ways seven years later, it was only a few months before I succumbed to Eric's charms, alternately enjoying and refusing them, pushing him away and punishing him for wanting too much, too soon. We endured three years of yo-yo dating, with him wanting so badly to make the relationship work and me wanting so badly...to be single.

I nearly laughed out loud now, thinking how deeply I'd been wallowing in my singlehood lately. For so long, I had wanted to just live as the strong, independent girl I felt at my core. Now I thought that I had maybe tossed away my last opportunity to be with a sane, willing, and attractive man. "It's just that it's been *forever*. And, you know, I'm thirty-six now. Everyone I'm into is already married. With a baby. It's not exactly the best age to be single. I mean, I'm thirty-six— what the fuck? How did this happen? Of course everyone is married. My mom was getting *divorced* when she was my age. I think that's what I have to do now: just wait for everyone to start getting divorced."

AJ was looking at me with a mix of sympathy and humor. "Aim, gimme a break. You're beautiful, smart, talented, funny—any guy would be so lucky to date you. I mean, you're living in *Paris!* You're so cool!"

"Ugh, whatever. I wasn't looking for a pity party," I said, the echo of her last words making me feel both proud and freaked out. "I mean, thank you, as always, for your kind words. But I'm sort of over thinking and talking about it." And it was true. I was tired of dissecting my single status. Everyone in New York kept asking me about the men in Paris—Were they flirtatious? Good kissers? Did they all sport moustaches and berets?—and I had absolutely nothing to report. I'd had a couple drunken make-out sessions in my six months, but not one single date. I didn't even have a crush on anyone. I felt old, shriveled up, and invisible. "Let's talk about something else." I changed the subject. "When are you going to come back to Paris? I found a good place where we can go dancing."

—— ✳ ——

I squeezed in as many of these heartfelt, honest, and cathartic conversations with AJ as I could in my remaining days in New York. But I also had to share her time with her new love. So much had changed since I had been gone, and not just certain restaurants losing their cachet or macaron cafés rising from nothing like properly whipped egg whites.

As I packed up for my return to Paris, I realized it was time to let go of New York for a while. That all the things I had always loved about the city still existed, but, after having lived abroad, I had a new perspective on them. Perhaps less kind and forgiving. It was a little alienating, and more than a little heartbreaking, to realize that everyone and everything was moving on (and moving to Brooklyn) without me. But it was also okay. Now I had Paris.

Just as Parisians are in the midst of a cupcake frenzy, New Yorkers are scooping up macarons like there's no demain. For flavors as inventive as Pierre Hermé's, try DessertTruck Works on the Lower East Side, which offers seasonal varieties like butternut squash and blackberry and Maker's Mark. Beautiful classics—lemon, salted caramel, pistachio— can be found nearby at Bisous Ciao. You can trot yourself around to any of the French masters, like François Payard, Bouchon Bakery, and La Maison du Chocolat. But best of all, you can see what all the French fuss is about: Ladurée made its New York debut in the summer of 2011.

Because the precious little double-decker bites of joy are so iconic in Paris, it goes without saying that you'll see them everywhere, not just at the powerhouses Pierre Hermé and Ladurée. I never really sampled the ones at the neighborhood boulangeries, but I did find macaron heaven at Jonathan Blot's Acide in the 17e, Arnaud Delmontel in the 9e, and, once again, Jean-Paul Hévin in the 1er (the man can do no wrong in my book).

CRUMBLING OVER PERFECTION

For months, I had been positively gushing about life in Paris: how charming the square-shaped trees were and how exquisite the gold-tipped ironwork; how graceful the seventeenth-century *hôtel particuliers* and enviable the French women's legs; how sweet the strawberries and how divine the wine. I think you could say I'd been prattling on ad nauseam about how everything in Paris was just...*perfect.*

As if.

After my visit to New York, accompanied as it was with my obnoxious "everything's better in Paris" attitude, karma caught up with me. Sure, my new home was beautiful and romantic and lovely and amazing, with delicious *boulangeries* and pâtisseries filled with delicately dreamy *viennoiserie* and *gâteaux* on each and every corner.

But it was also frustrating as hell.

For my new Parisian life, sadly, wasn't always spent sipping champagne on Ogilvy's rooftop with its prime views of the Eiffel Tower and l'Arc de Triomphe. Nor did every day contain a blessed visit to a sleek new chocolatier where three-tiered fountains spouted molten cocoa for all. In fact, since summer turned to fall, the fantasy faded. Just as I had felt like a foreigner a few weeks ago in New York, being back in Paris made me hyperaware of a giant cultural divide. I was surprised—and, *oui*, a little hurt—to see that my new love did in fact have faults. And I didn't like the taste of things to come.

———— ✳ ————

My return from New York in September coincided with *la rentrée*—a time of magical new beginnings in Paris that's like "back to school" in the States, only bigger and more profound. Beyond just kids getting new pencil boxes and corduroys after a summer of catching fireflies and building campfires, it's *the* season of renewal. Change is embraced and celebrated by every proud citizen; it's a fêted homecoming for the entire city that is returning to work after spending August frolicking *à la plage*—unless, of course, they were like me and the Louis Vuitton team, who toiled not only the entire sacred heat-filled month, but every weekend of it too.

To be fair, disillusionment started creeping in before my

New York visit and *la rentrée* to Paris. Summer had barely kicked off when Vuitton announced they wanted a new website—a major undertaking—and they were also opening the opportunity up to other agencies. We would continue to do their existing digital advertising, but we'd also have to defend the account and prove ourselves worthy of the additional project. In other words, we were in pitch mode. *Au revoir, summer.*

But we weren't just called upon to defend our work (and honor)—we did it gagged and blindfolded. On our knees, with our hands tied behind our backs. For the very same day I learned about the pitch, Fred, the creative director who recruited me and brought me over to Paris, announced he was packing up his home and family and moving to New York himself. He was out of there. Ogilvy's worldwide creative director subsequently bounced back and forth between New York and Paris all summer to help fill the void, but it was still a devastating loss. Personally, it felt weird that the guy who was, in effect, responsible for my being in Paris was leaving so soon after my arrival. And on the work front, I couldn't help but think the creative director's departure didn't bode well for our chances of winning the Louis Vuitton relaunch.

I think it's fair to say I felt jilted by all this un-Gallic behavior. My visions of canal-side picnics in August were cruelly dashed, to say nothing of the chocolate éclairs heavy with custard, the buttery brioches that begged to be pinched and devoured, and raspberry tarts with their plump berries perfectly fanned out across precious beds of *crème pâtissière* and moist *pâte sablée* crusts that would have to go untasted while I was at the office.

I mean, sure, it was fun and sexy to write about supple leather handbags and glittery cruise collections designed for fabulous jet-setters who needed wardrobes for their two-week romps in St. Bart's and Gstaad. It was exciting to dream up new ways of bringing the luxury brand's rich and impressive 155-year-old history to life in ways never envisioned. It's true—working on an account like Louis Vuitton is the stuff copywriters kill (and, worse, backstab!) for. But even so, I'd opt for the relatively modest pleasure of biting into a piping hot Nutella crepe out on boulevard Saint-Germain over drafting clever headlines any day of the week. Especially a Saturday or Sunday.

Luckily, I had squeezed in some trips back in May and June. In fact, May is riddled with national holidays in France and the way they fell on the calendar that year meant three long weekends in one month. I took full advantage.

My first journey outside the city was when Michael and I road-tripped to the Loire Valley, spending two days touring chateaux and sipping Vouvray, the local sparkling wine. Then I took a solo trip to Biarritz, a kickass beach town near the border of Spain that's known for its big waves and surf tournaments. Though I can barely swim, I love the salty air and laidback vibe of coastal towns and Biarritz proved to be both mellow and sophisticated. On one of the days, I went to the town's incredible *marché*—another French orgy of bread, cheese, pastries, fruit, vegetables, wine, meat, and seafood—and bought a beautiful hunk of *pain aux céréales* (fresh, dense multigrain bread), *brebis* (a local sheep's milk cheese), and strawberries (so sweet) so I could picnic on the beach while watching the surfers. The other days were spent sampling regional sweets like the *gâteau Basque* and *pâte d'amandes*. The former was a dry, circular shortbread cake filled with cherry preserves, the latter, basically marzipan. It came in infinite flavors, from raspberry to lemon to pine nut to chocolate, and was sometimes sliced and packaged like chocolate bars, and sometimes cut into bite-sized pieces, rolled in sugar and sold in bags like bonbons. It was delicious both ways.

And in June, Melanie, one of my single girlfriends from New York, met me for a week on the Côte d'Azur. We explored breathtaking mountain villages and seaside trails, walking up hills and down crooked streets. We sauntered along the famous *croisette*, or waterfront boulevard, in Cannes and overindulged in fresh fish and creamy gelato in the old town of Nice. We wore bikinis and sundresses and danced on tables and drank Pastis. By the end of the week, I felt as young and free as a college student again. Every trip I took made me fall more in love with the French countryside, and it seemed just plain cruel that I couldn't spend the entire summer enjoying foreign escapades.

But there were some silver linings to being at the office so much. I was finally bonding with my Louis Vuitton team, and even meeting other people. On one of the brilliant July Saturdays we were stuck at the office, I met Jo, an Australian art director who had been with Ogilvy for a couple years. I had taken a break to go up to the rooftop and cheer on the international Tour de France cyclists making their final laps up and down the Champs-Élysées (another good thing about having to work that day, I guess: having a prime view of this prestigious event). Jo was doing the same, but she was making a day of it, there on Ogilvy's terrace with an expat gang and cache of picnic goodies.

I had been peripherally aware of Jo's cool, street-smart style around the office but had never had the occasion to chat with her. That day, sensing a kindred spirit, she introduced herself and insisted I have a spot of her rosé—a friendly and generous gesture that was not lost on me. Before I retreated inside to work, we agreed to meet for lunch when my schedule settled down. After slaving away all summer, we—Jo and I—did have lunch, and we—Ogilvy—were awarded the site relaunch. Our days of summer drudgery paid off.

Before work got too busy again, I wanted to tap into *la rentrée's* electric energy and make all kinds of declarations for growth and betterment—the kind of optimistic gestures that Oprah would have inspired back home with her January issue of *O Magazine*. With revving scooters buzzing in the city again like swarms of angry bees, and chic *mamans* bustling about in their flouncy skirts, escorting their adorable kids who had better wardrobes than me, I was determined. It was time to set some goals. At the top of my list: study more French, take on additional freelance writing assignments, and make new friends.

It was time to see how deeply my roots might grow in my new home.

I fancied myself *une vraie Parisienne*, coming back from New York and embracing this social norm. But practically as I was drafting my to-do list, I lost my motivation. Suddenly nothing moved or inspired me. And instead of boning up on possessive pronouns and breaking into all the American publications like I had vowed to do, I found myself avoiding my French workbook like *la grippe* and procrastinating on the very few writing assignments I did have.

Even my passion for the Vélib's waned. With the whole city's return from the beach, the boulevards were suddenly choked with Peugeots and Renaults and their thick diesel fumes. Besides, the sun was setting earlier and earlier and it was usually dusk now when I left work. The streets felt precarious, and I didn't have the heart or nerves for bicycling. I found myself in a cloud of paralysis and dourness. I felt tired, achy, stressed, and short-tempered—not exactly the magnificent *rentrée* I had envisioned.

———— ✳ ————

One thing that kept me going were my evenings and weekends, when I wandered the city. I grew starry-eyed, ogling the floor-length gowns and impossibly high *talons hauts* through the windows of rue Saint-Honoré's chichi boutiques, and was blissfully happy hand-picking my peaches and leeks from the markets on rues Cler and d'Aligre. It thrilled me to count the different angels, lords, and gargoyles that decorated the apartment façades and the way some people grew veritable jungles on their four-foot-wide balconies. I adored exploring the different neighborhoods, with all the cute little *cul de sacs* and ancient *boulangeries*, and I'd inevitably get lost, which would make the discovery of a random eclectic boutique or lonesome park all the more magical. Being part of Paris's daily beats and rhythms was why I was there.

But actually, as my ever-increasing assignments and deadlines at Ogilvy reminded me, the reason I was in Paris was to…*work*. Even easing back into regular life after cranking on the pitch all summer, I was pulling longer, more intense hours than I had in New York. When I had arrived in the springtime, I was shocked to discover that most people were at the office until well past 7:00 p.m. every night. But now, 8:00 p.m. was becoming my habitual departure time. The thirty-five-hour French workweek I had arrived believing would be mine was nothing but a myth. And to add insult to injury, I knew the days could have been shorter if only we didn't have these absurd meetings in which my colleagues flexed their excellent verbalization skills, pontificating and deliberating forever and ever without ever really concluding anything. The French loved to hear themselves talk. (Or, as Steve Martin said, in better humor than me, "Boy, those French. They have a different word for everything.") Plus, it had been two months since Fred and Isa had left and they still hadn't been replaced. We were understaffed, and I was juggling a workload meant for three. In New York, my creative directors would have called in a small army of freelancers. In Paris, my inquiries about replacements and requests for help were met with utter silence.

I had grinned and borne the intense pace every perfectly sunny weekend in August. But as the days got darker with autumn, so did my mood. I was being given new, increasingly demanding tasks—drafting strategy decks, creating social media plans, writing client presentations—and never knew if it was because a writer's role was different in Paris than in New York, if agency life was different in Paris than in New York, or if it was just because I was getting screwed. In any case, I was on my own. I didn't have a boss to ask these questions, and I could hardly say no to the work. I had to suck it up.

Finally, when one of the responsibilities that was fobbed off on me was entering one of our websites into an award show, I had to put my foot down. This task required me to write a script for a case study. But the agency had a dedicated public relations woman for handling things just like that. The account team was four people strong, and there was exactly one copywriter—me, who had tons of her own work to do, thank you very much. Award show entries were something I did at my very first job in San Francisco as a creative *assistant*. Had they really transferred me, an associate creative director, thirty-six hundred miles to write case studies? And had I really traded in my easy-breezy life in New York to work like a dog in Paris?

The case study was killing me. Whenever I presented a script to the team, someone would weigh in with a new opinion, and I would get sent in a whole new direction. It was a classic case of trying to hit a moving bull's-eye because no one had bothered to figure out the strategy or direction. Meanwhile, my real projects were piling up. New programs and products still had to be promoted. There was website maintenance, plus the relaunch project was gearing up. I was also spending more time recruiting and interviewing copywriter candidates to join the team. I was desperate for reinforcements.

There was no chain of command and no urgency, just a mind-numbing desire to keep talking without ever doing, all of which was slowly driving me mad, and—if it meant having the process and guidance I had once enjoyed in the American workplace—it was even making me want to leave the fabulous Beaux-Arts *bureau* on the Champs-Élysées and go back to the crummy corporate offices in the hellhole known as Times Square. I was definitely ready to pack it up when I found myself in a windowless conference room at six o'clock on a Friday night, absolutely fatigued and frustrated, with my account team staring at me blankly as only the French can do.

"I don't get it," I said, looking down at my marked-up script. "I don't get it, I don't get it," I numbly repeated myself. Even though our team communicated in English, I had been finding myself so flustered and exhausted lately that I might as well have been trying to speak Swahili. They were now steering me down yet another new path, which would require another half day of work. "But why am *I* doing this?" I asked, aware that I sounded horribly whiny. But, *God*, it felt great to introduce my inner six-year-old to the team and whine for the first time in six months!

"You're the writer," Cedric calmly pointed out—like, *duh*. Every time I voiced a doubt or raised a question, he had the most brilliant way of plainly explaining that, no really, A could be put on the back burner and B didn't matter, and that C was doing D, and all I really needed to do was focus on E because, really, F and everything else was totally manageable for one person and there was really no reason for me to freak out. At all. Silly American. Silly girl.

But this whole situation was just ridiculous. It seemed like more than just a cultural difference. This was bullshit. This was *so! not! my! job!*

I looked desperately around the small, soulless room. It was four account people versus one writer. Nobody wanted responsibility for the project, but I had no one on my side. No one to back me up. I had been trying so hard to keep it together and assimilate. Trying to ace every assignment. Trying to figure out the printers and scanners, agency policies and processes, my colleagues and clients. I was still trying to master a French keyboard. So as I looked at my team looking at me as if I were the crazy one that night, I did the only thing possible: I lost it.

— ✳ —

I remember when an ex-boyfriend in New York called me a "control freak"; I roared with laughter. *Moi?* A control freak? It struck me as the funniest thing in the world. For about three seconds, until I realized he was right. I do sort of like things my way. I had this same tragic *aha* moment when Melissa used the P-word on me.

"How did it make you feel?" she asked the next day, sipping her Negroni at the teeny café table where we were seated. "Not being perfect?"

With every conversation, Mel and I realized we were virtually the same exact person, born five years apart. She was also from New York and had moved to Paris at the age of thirty-six. She had once worked in the ad industry and understood its inanity. While I was currently suffering through writer's block with my freelance articles, she was doing the same with a novel. She was single and of a certain age and was quite happy and comfortable with it. We both loved Fleetwood Mac and The Jesus and Mary Chain, peonies and vintage YSL, interior design and shabby-chic aesthetics. We were both sensitive and sentimental, and yet strong and independent. Together, we didn't care how ridiculous we looked dancing and miming "YMCA" in a crowded bar full of strangers. Sometimes our systems were so in tune, we discovered we both suffered from homesickness, ennui, cramps, or diarrhea at the very same time, despite having not seen each other for days. Luckily for me, she was the one with a few more years of experience and could transmit her lessons to me—even if I didn't always want to hear it.

"I'm sorry?" I sputtered. "You think I'm trying to be a perfectionist or something? I'm just trying to do my *job*!"

"Listen, bunny, I have been there. I know what you're going through, and trust me when I say to you that you simply cannot do it all: the work, plus the freelance, the socializing, the blogging..." For by that point, my blogging about the ecstasy and agony of expat life in Paris had become a mild addiction with a public following. It often kept me up well past my bedtime. "You will have to let go of something." Her hand was gently rubbing my shoulder as she forced me to make eye contact. "You can't keep biting off more than you can chew. There are worse things than not being perfect."

"What are you even talking about? I'm not trying…I'm not trying to be…perfect!" With the words finally out, I could feel tears prickling my eyes. She had struck a chord. I wanted to be liked and respected by my colleagues. I wanted to prove myself invaluable to the Louis Vuitton team. I wanted to do great work, not only because that's what they brought me there to do, but also because I felt I had to prove myself as an American, as a woman, as…Amy. *Little Miss Parfait.* I wanted to do it all. And Melissa could see right through me.

Later that day, after Melissa had gotten me through my second breakdown in as many days and sent me off with the big American hug I needed, I stood outside the new *haute pâtisserie* Hugo et Victor, genuflecting at one of my holy altars of perfection. It all started to come together. The meticulously measured layers of mousse and ganache atop praline puff pastry of Jean-Paul Hévin's choco-passion cake. The sublimely symmetrical circles of individual choux pastries filled with beautiful, billowy *praliné crème* that was La Pâtisserie des Rêves's Paris-Brest. The flawless fondant finishes of Arnaud Delmontel's kaleidoscopic cakes. All of those pretty Parisian pastries made life seem so lovely and wonderful and…perfect. And it hit me like a banana cream pie in the face: *I can't stand for things to be messy.*

I think it's a divorced child syndrome: if the apartment is clean and tidy, then everything will be all right. If my closet and checkbook are organized, I am in total control of my life. If the party spread is arranged just so, then everyone is guaranteed to have a great time. All of my new life's uncertainty and hardship, of struggling with a foreign language and different culture, of never knowing the right thing to do or the proper thing to say, all of this…this…*messiness*—it was throwing me for a loop.

But if I truly was a control freak like my ex-boyfriend claimed, then shouldn't I be able to, well, *control* things? Didn't I have the power to make the changes I needed? I could do something about these feelings of frustration and inadequacy and steer myself to a better place. Starting now.

Standing before the sparkling cake-filled window of Hugo et Victor, I conjured all of my willpower and turned away from its prim, proper, pretty, pastel creations in defiance. *Not today, my lovelies.* It was time for something messy.

—— ✳ ——

By its very nature, the crumble is a hot, heaping mess: an oozing fruit base, a haphazardly scattered topping, and a texture that deliciously swings from tender to crunchy. The fruit lends tartness, the streusel topping adds sweetness—one without the other is like peanut butter without Fluff, cake without frosting, an Oreo denuded of its white cream center. And if you dare try making the crumble a perfect *haut* dessert rather than the warm pile of comfort food that it is, you're likely to fall flat on your face—sort of like I had done a few months back, tumbling down the stairs in my Robert Clergeries.

With such a pedigree, it's no wonder the crumble is a traditional British dessert. The Brits are a no-nonsense bunch. They created the crumble during World War II when pie crust ingredients were being rationed. Forgoing the base and just warming up stewed fruit that was sprinkled with a mixture of margarine, flour, and sugar on top kept everyone as sated as possible during tough times.

I had succumbed to the charms of blueberry cobbler at Make My Cake, the bustling bakery in Harlem that's been serving Southern specialties like hot cross buns and red velvet cake, made from protected family recipes, since 1995.

"A *crumble?* What's that? You mean the cobbler?" the guy behind the counter giggled at me when I first ordered the dessert by the wrong name. Over time, in different parts of the country, Americans have adopted different versions of *le crumble*. There's the crisp, which is essentially the same sweet-tart formula as the British crumble. Brown betties, which feature buttered crumb bits that are baked *between* the layers of fruit—the fruit most commonly being apples. And cobblers, traditionally Southern deep-dish desserts with a pie crust on bottom and either a thick biscuit or pie crust on top. Make My Cake had giant pans of wickedly sweet, syrupy pie filling covered in lattice shortbread crusts. Once the guy knew what I wanted, he slopped it into a plastic to-go container, no thought to its presentation. But it didn't matter; it didn't affect the taste. It was the kind of dessert that was so bad, it was good. It coated my belly. Filled me up. And felt like a sloppy-sweet embrace. Now that I was in Paris, I needed a hit of that love.

— ✳ —

One day on my previous summer's Tour du Chocolat, as I was coasting along rue de l'Université, I had nearly flown over my Vélib's handlebars after slamming on the brakes. On this quiet stretch of the seventh arrondissement, a notoriously Anglophone area, I had been distracted—very distracted—by a double-decker table filled with magnificent cakes and tarts I saw in a small tea salon's window. An older gentleman must have witnessed my clumsy act of admiration from inside for, as I was pulling out my notebook to jot down the salon's name, straddling the heavy and awkward bicycle, he appeared from nowhere and gallantly handed me a business card: *Les Deux Abeilles*, The Two Bees. I thanked him before speeding off on my chocolaty way, vowing to return.

Two years later, I conjured the name of the tearoom. I

dragged my ass back on a Vélib'. And I peddled across town, happy to see that Les Deux Abeilles was as sweet as my memory made it out to be. It had a fusty charm, with floral wallpaper and antique furniture, and vases of flowers and potted plants lent color and freshness. The two dining rooms were flooded with sunshine from an overhead skylight and French doors that opened onto the sidewalk. It felt as comfortable and safe as if Anne and Valeria Arella, the mother-daughter team who ran it, had invited me into their own country home. Just as decadent too. I immediately saw that, in addition to the display of tarts, crumbles, scones, and cakes in the window that had caused my near wipeout way back when, there was a whole other table laden with irresistible sweets.

I had finished my *omelette nature* with its perfectly dressed greens and had been eyeing both tables, mulling over my choices throughout the entire lunch. "Would you mind explaining what the desserts are?" I asked the very pretty and polished Valeria. She wore white jeans, a camel-colored cashmere v-neck and her hair in an elegant ponytail, and I supposed it was only by running such a popular spot six days a week that she remained so thin.

"Bien sûr," she responded. Despite the lunchtime bustle, she personally guided me to the front of the dining room, bringing me face to face with tens of thousands of calories.

"This is a pear-praline *clafoutis*," she began, pointing to the pudding-like dessert that looked like a sweet, crustless quiche flipped on its top. "This is a peach tarte, and this is a plum tarte," she continued identifying the desserts, one by one.

"Do you make them all here?" I asked.

"Yes, we are like acrobats in the kitchen, it's so small. *C'est pas confortable*," Valeria shared with a shrug and small smile. She told me they had been making the same recipes since she and her mother, the "two bees," opened the tea-room in 1985. Then she got back to the business at hand. "This here's our lemon meringue tarte, this is a chocolate fondant cake, this chocolate fondant has praline, and this one is chocolate brownie." She then guided me over to the other table, where my greedy eyes grew even larger as she continued the parade of possibilities. Scones, tarte tatin, cheesecake, and, finally, she finished with what I had been yearning for: "And the crumble today is rhubarb-apple." She turned to me. "I'll give you a minute to decide," she smiled, walking off to the kitchen.

I lingered at the table, eyeing the golden brown topping of the crumble, clattering tea cups and intimate conversations dancing in the background. It was similar to Make My Cake's cobbler in that it was a giant dish of oozing fruit concealed by bits of topping—exactly what I had come for. Yet it was unmistakably French. While it was indeed messier than the *gâteaux* I had fallen for elsewhere around Paris, Les Deux Abeilles's crumble, presented in a round white porcelain dish, was still more refined. It looked thick and sweet and crunchy. I could practically taste the buttery bits and jammy fruit converging in a chaotic mix of flavors and textures in my mouth.

But now that pear-praline *clafoutis* was waving to me from across the room like a dense and eggy terrine from heaven. And the tall, airy wisps on the lemon meringue were tempting me, as well as the towering cheesecake, fluffier than the versions back home, with more finesse. Molten chocolate cake is never the wrong choice, I was rationalizing to myself, when Valeria returned. "*Alors*, what will it be?"

I gazed up at her comforting presence. "I'll take the crumble, please."

After my laborious decision, I was relieved to discover I had been right to stick with my original intentions. Five minutes later, a generous slice of rhubarb-apple crumble arrived, warmed in the small kitchen and served with a side of fresh cream, whipped staunchly into a thick, puffy cloud. I sat for a minute, contemplating the crumble's imperfect bumps and dull brown color. The pale pink and sometimes green slices of rhubarb poked out of the sides and lumps of rogue topping decorated my plate. Where the crumble had baked against the dish, a sticky crust of caramelized fruit juice and sugar had formed. It looked like a tarte that had done a somersault in its pastry box and arrived bruised and battered. There was nothing perfect about it. Except its bright flavors. Except its comforting warmth. Except that it was exactly what I wanted and needed. I savored each juicy-crunchy bite. It was wonderful.

— ✳ —

I went back to the office on Monday, embracing my imperfect job, my imperfect situation, and my own imperfections. All those months, I had been idealizing all the perfect little cakes, just as I had been Paris, as a city and as my new home. And I saw that nobody was expecting me to be perfect—except me. So I couldn't wow my colleagues with French fluency. So maybe I wasn't going to kick ass on everything the Louis Vuitton team asked me to do. And so what if my weekend's dessert discovery looked more like a third grader's bake sale contribution than the picture-perfect cakes in the windows of Hugo et Victor? Really, *so what?* It was time to be more open: to the unexpected, the unfamiliar, and, especially, the imperfect.

MORE
Sweet Spots
ON THE
MAP

Crumbles are curiously popular in Paris. They're not only common dessert options at restaurants and tearooms, but they're also often made at home for Sunday dinners and sold at boulangeries. *Sometimes they're baked in big sheets and sliced and served in rectangular portions. Me? I like the tidy, little circular pistachio and cherry crumbles served at Eric Kayser.*

Crisps and crumbles make an occasional appearance on New York dessert menus (the always-divine Gramercy Tavern comes to mind), but they're harder to come by than in Paris. When they are served at bakeries, it's usually a seasonal thing offered around the autumn holidays. But Little Pie Company makes a delightful sour cream apple walnut pie whose streusel topping is awfully close to a good crumble. And it's served year-round.

—[C H A P T E R 7]—

CAKES TO BE LOVED
AND CHERISHED

I may have been embracing my imperfections, but the Parisian men weren't. I mean, forget Robert Doisneau café cuddles, moonlight strolls along the Seine, and dancers twirling beneath streetlamps glowing rose. My dating life so far exhibited none of the romantic trappings that the black-and-white posters on my college dorm walls had promised me sixteen years ago. The sad fact was, it reminded me more of my college boyfriend's dorm room poster of Larry, Moe, and Curly: funny, ridiculous, and in a set of three.

My first date came about, unsurprisingly, after a night out with Michael. As my quintessential bachelor friend, we had an implicit agreement to be each other's wingmen when we met for happy hours and nightcaps.

"Sooo? Did you get his number?" he trilled toward the

end of a night at Experimental, one of the city's chicest—nay, one of the city's *only*—cocktail bars, which had been started a year and a half earlier by three natty friends. It was more East Village speakeasy than common *comptoir* or ubiquitous café, giving a mostly international crowd a sophisticated place to drink and dance. Not even two blocks away from my tree house, I was lucky to claim this little taste of home as "my" neighborhood bar.

"*Oui, oui*, and I gave him mine," I yawned, always staying out later than I should with Michael. Even though I wasn't particularly charmed by the tall, skinny, Swedish trust fund baby I had chatted with for forty minutes, I was determined to live by my new Paris motto: *Be open. Say yes.* So I agreed to meet the beanpole for a drink the following week. Michael and I high-fived.

— ✳ —

The night hardly started auspiciously. Alec, the Swedish bean-pole, suggested we meet outside a pub on rue Saint-Denis. Now, unless you're walking around with a penis, rue Saint-Denis is not the most desirable place—an infamous stretch of dingy sex shops, seedy massage parlors, and fifty-year-old hookers with vinyl boots and basketball-sized implants loitering in doorways. I tried to keep my chin up after fifteen minutes of waiting for Alec, lecherous men muttering and blowing kisses in my face the whole time. It was one of the few times I was relieved, not amiss, that I couldn't understand what was being said to me. I was about to text and cancel when the beanpole jogged up, shoulder-length brown hair flapping in the wind. *What was I thinking, agreeing to this?* But as suddenly as the thought entered my mind, I squashed it, trying to embrace the night with my new optimism. (Be open! Say yes!)

Once we were settled inside a nearby bar with gin and tonics—his eighth by the smell of it—Alec rapidly progressed from small talking to flirting to seducing. Within minutes, he leaned over and just started making out with me. No attempt at warming things up. No soft *"hello, you"* kiss. Just a full on make-out attack. And he wasn't a good kisser. That said, I must admit I was a little flattered. This kid was probably twelve years younger than me, and I hadn't even been sure if our drink, when arranged the week before, was intended to be platonic or romantic. After my months of lonely moments, I was finally on a date. So I went with it, still being open! Saying yes!

"So," he sat back, all smug and smiley, his concave brown chest peeking out from the crisp shirt that was unbuttoned one more button than it should have been. "Should we go home now or meet my friends at a club?"

It had been a long time since someone rendered me speechless, and I laughed in his face. "Um, right," I said, wiping my lips dry. "Why don't we join your friends."

My bullshit sensor on high alert, we left to ostensibly go to this club, but along the way, he dragged us into a brightly lit, sadly empty bar with thumping music. It was then I realized how horrendous French music is. Sure, they had Serge in the sixties, Air in the nineties, and add me to the list of Phoenix fans. But otherwise, the outdated house music and cheesy crooners that permeate are embarrassingly unhip.

Alec marched up to the bartender like he owned the joint and ordered himself, *only* himself, a drink, and though he was generous enough to let me take sips of his vodka and mint liquor, I declined after the first sip, having gagged at what tasted like tainted mouthwash. I found myself in that mute role again, not so much because I couldn't understand the language—I just didn't get this guy's behavior. I was simultaneously fascinated and horrified as he kept leaning over and mauling me. What can I say? It was one of those things where I was so aware of the absurdity of the situation, but I didn't care. (Be open! Say yes!)

But then things just started getting dumb. "Don't you want to go home with an arrogant bastard?" he asked, grinding against the bar and flipping his hair behind his ear. "Don't you want to be able to tell your friends you slept with a hot Parisian?" Incapable of a kind or clever response, I just smiled and shook my head. He switched tactics. "Okay, time for a shot!"

"Yeah, that's not going to happen, Alec." Finally, my senses were coming back to me. The comedy routine had gone on long enough. "It's time for me to call it a night."

"What?" He was incredulous. And I was incredulous that he was incredulous. "C'mon. Let's do a shot. What do you want? Whiskey? Tequila?"

"No, seriously, I'm going to go now."

"No, wait. Just walk me to this club where my friends are," he said, apparently no longer interested in who I was but only in what I could do for him. He was furiously texting on his mobile. "They'll charge me if I'm alone, but not if you're with me. So come with me, it's really close, and *then* you can go home."

It was 1:15 on a Wednesday night. I had to meet Josephine for my French lesson at 8:30 the following morning. I was done. "Hmm, that's tempting. But still, I'm going home." I was making my way to the door, over his protestations. "Thanks, um, for an, um...see ya!" Having reached the door, I bolted midsentence and started running through the cobblestoned streets without so much as a glance over my shoulder. When I was safely back in my tree house, I noticed my phone ringing. Alec wanted to come over. In disbelief—at his audacity and because I couldn't figure out how to turn my phone off (French wasn't my only challenge; I was an iPhone girl back in New York, and I couldn't quite figure out the BlackBerry the Paris office gave me)—I hung up without any pretenses of *politesse*, dislodged the phone's battery, and crawled into bed.

The next morning, I had *twelve* missed calls. And when I hopped off my Vélib' outside Ladurée, ready for my French lesson, the phone rang again. It was the Swedish beanpole, oblivious, still wanting to know if he should come over.

My first date in Paris: strike one.

———— ✹ ————

About a month later, I connected with a Frenchman—a *sane* Frenchman. I went to a Pretenders concert, giddy about seeing one of my favorite all-time bands in my favorite all-time city. I had been to two great shows since arriving in Paris, both at incredibly intimate venues that would have sold out in, well, a New York minute, back home. My music karma was good, and I had big expectations for the night. It was an unusually steamy night, and beads of sweat were already tickling my back before I entered Élysée Montmartre, a two-hundred-year-old music venue that had hosted everyone from David Bowie to Robbie Williams. The French are infamous for not investing in air-conditioning—but I thought a major music venue where twelve hundred people cram into one room might be different. It wasn't; it was going to be a hot night. Weaving through the crowd, I found an open pocket and noticed a very cute guy in a simple white button-down, perfectly worn Levi's, and closely cropped salt-and-pepperish hair nearby. He was also alone.

More and more people started filing in around us, the

air getting stickier with every one of them. I was as acutely aware that I was standing next to a single, attractive guy as I was that my naturally curly hair was undoubtedly getting bigger and frizzier by the minute. Chrissie Hynde and the rest of the band had taken the stage, starting with "Break Up the Concrete." I needed to seize the opportunity before I had an afro.

Striking up conversation with strangers has never been my forte. In New York, AJ was always there to loosen things up and give me a jolt of confidence, telling me how funny I was or that I was having a good hair night. She encouraged me to make eye contact, not put pressure on myself, and to just enjoy meeting people, with no expectation for the outcome. So I kept thinking: *What would AJ do?* As I was channeling my best friend in New York, Chrissie was snarling on stage: "Il fait chaud! Merde!" I cracked up with the rest of the roaring crowd at her ability to say it was bloody hot in there like a badass Frenchie. Then I made my move.

"Elle est la mieux," I shouted to Salt-and-Pepper, letting him know I thought she was the coolest chick going.

"Oui, oui," he smiled back at me. Okay, so maybe he had been looking at me out of the corner of his eye, too. "Oui…"

"As-tu déjà vu?" My French was laughable, but I wasn't backing down now that I had successfully made contact.

"Oui, trois fois," he smiled at me again. What a great smile. "Toi?" We exchanged adoration for our mutual idol the rest of the show, in between jumping around to "Message of Love" and singing "Brass in Pocket" at the top of our lungs. As we were getting herded out of the sweaty venue ninety minutes later, he asked me if I wanted to get a drink. I did. So we did!

We climbed the hill to rue des Abbesses, a street in Montmartre jammed with classic cafés—the kind Robert Doisneau would have photographed—my stomach aflutter for the first time since coming to Paris. We sat down and the hours ticked by as we talked about music, traveling, France, and politics. While he did most of the talking, I was still proud I was keeping up and following, oh, about 40 percent of what he was saying. Although, toward the end, he did get very French on me—talking superfast with *beaucoup* gesticulations to emphasize his points. That's when I began to check out, again faced with the reality that French people really like to hear themselves pontificate. After shutting down the café, we exchanged numbers—and names, which we hadn't until that point. Frank. What a nice name. What a nice night.

The following evening, when I hadn't heard from him, I told myself I could text him. *Pourquoi pas?* AJ would. But things had started on a French foot. It seemed too ugly-American to do that. So I waited. For nothing, as it turned out. Josephine was certain the reason I hadn't heard from him was because he was married. She pointed out that he lived in *les banlieues* and had a daughter and had probably just come in for the night to see the concert. So confident was my plump, schoolmarmish tutor whose every word of French I clung to that a week later, I had to concede. Strike two.

——— ✳ ———

Meanwhile, after a lifetime of wondering who "the one" would be, AJ finally knew. My best friend was getting married.

"Hi, Aim. Call me when you can," her voice mail said. "I want to tell you something." It was a short and simple message, but I knew. I could hear the restrained giddiness in her voice. Since meeting Mitchell the previous month, I knew he was different from the other New York clowns. I called her immediately.

"So, tell me," I baited. "What's up?" I felt compelled to let her know that I knew exactly what she was about to share. She started giggling the way she did when we lip-synced Duran Duran's "Wild Boys" back in 1984. Oh my, she had it bad. "You're engaged, aren't you?"

"Yessss!" she melted into the phone. For the next ten minutes, she recounted every detail of her night in the Meatpacking District, which started with Mitchell buying her a new dress at Diane von Furstenburg, then proceeded to a lovely dinner at Bagatelle, a moonlight walk on the High Line, bended knee proposal, a suite at the new Standard Hotel, champagne…

I stared out my window, looking across the zinc rooftops to Sacré-Coeur, glowing big and white up on Montmartre.

I felt strangely detached. Mostly it was because I was hearing AJ's happiness through a crummy little BlackBerry, in a rented apartment, in the middle of a foreign city. *How did I wind up here?* AJ and I had been attached at the hip for twenty-five years. And now for one of the biggest milestones in life, she was back home, and I was thirty-six hundred miles away from the excitement.

But it was also something else. As happy as I was for her, her engagement made my single status more conspicuous. It hadn't been that long since I arrived in Paris, all starry-eyed and buoyed by the confidence of being "a catch." Colleagues and acquaintances had told me being a foreigner was an asset in Paris. That my accent was "cute" and my expat status "exotic." But after months of hearing this and nothing but two dubious dates to back it up, I was beginning to wonder: was I going to strike out in the world's most lover-ly city? I wouldn't have admitted it to just anyone, but I had secretly dreamed of meeting a cute pastry chef and eating tarte tatin for the rest of my life. But the closest I was getting to romance was an old amputee in a wheelchair telling me I had *jolies jambes*. I may have pretty legs, but they weren't getting me anywhere. Out of the five of us best friends from high school, I was the last one standing—the only unattached one.

Getting engaged hadn't exactly been at the top of my to-do list. Ever since graduating from college, I had let my career dictate my path in life. With a New York agent and budding editorial career, the prospect of a fat book advance had prompted me to leave San Francisco—and Max—for Manhattan at the prime marrying age of twenty-nine. And now my advertising career had brought me to Paris at an age where the news programs and my outspoken aunts were telling me I'd better heed my biological clock, or else. Certainly, I had thought about love and marriage and babies over the years. It's just that how to get a byline in *Elle* magazine had always been a bigger deal than how to get a guy.

So a year ago, my single status wouldn't have bothered me one bit. It had become central to my identity and was normally such a source of pride. I protected my independence, enjoyed my freedom, and had done enough dating over the years that I didn't feel like a hopeless leper.

But something was triggered by AJ's engagement. She had been my steady companion through two and a half decades, across country borders, and despite our respective relationships. Now, she was going to be committing to someone else. I felt more alone than ever.

— ✳ —

"Uh, hel-lo? Being single in Paris is like having a social disease," Michael explained, dumbfounded he had to point out this very evident truth. "I mean, if you're not in a relationship, you might as well be dead." He paused, watching a guy in a manual wheelchair maneuver the crosswalk outside the window of Gaya Rive Gauche, Pierre Gagnaire's pricey seafood restaurant. "Or a paraplegic."

We were indulging in one of our regular lunch splurges, and I was whining, as I had been with increasing frequency, about my lack of dating opportunities. At least the restaurant was proving to be a winner, even if I wasn't. While perusing the menu, we indulged in crusty bread, served with both butter and olive oil—it's a rarity to get one or the other, much less both in Paris. We were also enjoying a beautiful *amuse-bouche* of octopus salad, which we speared with toothpicks, and a carafe of chilled Valflaunès Blanc. And the subsequent courses, right down to the chocolate praline cake served with rhubarb compote and salted caramel ice cream, were *fantastique*. But still, it had nothing on our previous lunch at Le Grand Vefour.

—— ✳ ——

The history of Le Grand Vefour, tucked inside the gardens of the Palais-Royal in the first arrondissement, goes back to King Louis XV's reign. It's legendary. Napoleon wooed Josephine there. Victor Hugo, Alexander Dumas, and Colette all dined there. It has three Michelin stars and a masterpiece of an eighteenth-century interior, complete with lush red velvet banquets, gilt trim, painted frescoes, crisp white linens, and silver vases skyrocketing with fresh flowers. It's an unforgettable experience before you even sit down to eat. But eat you do.

Michael and I had one o'clock reservations, and I ducked out of work inconspicuously enough. When I arrived at the restaurant, I joined my hungry friend at our table that afforded us a prime view of all the dining room's spectacles: the elaborate decanting of fine French wines, the delivery of the painstakingly constructed plates, and the meticulous choreography of the wait staff. There was a team of at least eight waiters, ranging in age from eighteen to eighty, each of whom clearly had his role (yes, *his*; there are only male waiters at Le Grand Vefour, and you can tell they're all proud to have worked there all their lives). More than once, one of the older gentlemen, in his dapper black suit, would catch me lustfully eyeing someone else's dessert and he'd joke, "Not yet," making me laugh.

We went for the three-course, €125 menu—obviously a splurge, and yet I barely batted an eye, seduced as I was by the restaurant's opulent setting. But the prix-fixe menu was also quite a value, considering it was really four courses once you factored in the biggest, most ridiculously decadent cheese course that came with it...or six courses, when you counted the two *amuses-bouches* that began the meal...or eight courses with the two side dishes served alongside our entrées...or *fourteen* courses with the dishes of complimentary *gelées*, caramels, chocolates, lemon cakes, and *petits fours* that came *in addition to* our dessert course. The meal was absolute madness. Absolute decadence. Absolute bliss. Each time someone from the cast of waiters approached our table to deliver a new plate, pour more wine, or just smile at us and make us feel like royalty—I wanted to give them another €10 in sheer gratitude. It was one of the richest dining experiences of my life.

Three and a half hours later, I was stuffed on French food and walking on air, though admittedly feeling a tinge of guilt for having been gone so long. As I approached the office, one of my colleagues who was on a smoke break looked at me knowingly. "Was it a good *baisenville*?" she asked. A *baisenville*, she had taught me only the week before, is slang for a "fuck in town." In other words, she had noticed how long I had been gone and naturally assumed I was enjoying some afternoon delight with my imaginary French lover. The way I had been struggling with cultural norms lately, it seemed like a midday romp would have been more acceptable than spending over three hours at lunch. So I did my best impersonation of a fabulous French woman, gave her a conspiratorial smile, and didn't say a word as I slipped back into the office.

—— ✳ ——

Back at Gaya Rive Gauche, Michael was still schooling me about dating in Paris. "Haven't you ever noticed that there's no *Sex and the City* equivalent here? It's not cool to be a single girl!" He sputtered on, "You've never noticed that everyone's a couple here? Whether they're happy or not? *Faithful* or not? It's all about image. The French are the biggest conformists in the world. They have to have their Sunday dinners with the family, someone to go on *les vacances* with, someone to split their baguettes with. Couples, man, couples! God forbid you make a dinner party awkward by forcing it to be an *odd* number." He couldn't stop himself now. "They're like monkeys," he continued. "They don't swing from their vines unless there's another one to jump onto. And since they've been palling around with their childhood friends forever, *that's* their pool of potential mates. They're not going to let *you* break in. The women would never have it, and the guys are too pussy." As he ranted on, everything started making sense.

Of course. How could I not have noticed these unspoken rules before? Everything in Paris, from the side-by-side café seats to the ping-pong tables in the parks, was arranged in pairs. I remembered being reduced to tears of humiliation at the Jardin des Tuileries carnival—not because I was a thirty-six-year-old at a carnival by myself, but because the operator of the *Grand Roue* made me stand in the sidelines for fifteen minutes like a naughty schoolgirl until another solo rider came along. I couldn't ride alone. Alone, *alone*.

I thought of the devout attentions of men at parties—until their girlfriends entered the room and led them away by the arm without so much as *bonsoir* to me. And the way my female colleagues took pride in going home every evening to make dinner for their boyfriends or husbands. At first, I thought it was sort of charming in a retro way.

No one back home would have ever admitted to such a traditional role. But now I saw that being in a relationship offered validation in Paris the same way having a successful career did in New York. Being half of a couple was the ticket to total self-worth.

"I mean, even the difference in the languages makes it clear," Michael was winding up, our bottle of wine empty, the dishes of caramel ice cream long since licked clean. "In English, 'single' sounds like you're ready to party. But *célibataire*? It sounds like you're entering a monastery."

Indeed. Once again, Michael had a point, and I was reminded that I wasn't finding my place in Paris. I was ready for a nap.

— ✸ —

In my short time in the City of Light, there was at least one man with whom I had become intimately acquainted: Pierre Hermé.

Variously coined "The Picasso of Pastry," "The King of Modern Pâtisserie," "The Pastry Provocateur," and "The Magician with Tastes," he's the rock star of the French pastry world. In a country that takes desserts as seriously as Americans take Hollywood relationships (that is to say, very), he has the respect and admiration of Paul Newman.

At the age of fourteen, in fact, Gaston Lenôtre of the famed Lenôtre Pâtisserie asked Pierre's father if he could apprentice Pierre. So at about the same age that I started whipping up Oreo blizzards for my illustrious career at Dairy Queen, Pierre began his in the French pastry world.

After five years at Lenôtre, at the spry age of nineteen, he became the head pastry chef. If you've ever seen the billowy white *gâteaux* or structurally perfect strawberry tarts from this Parisian landmark, you know how impressive this is. Later, he moved on to Fauchon, another top marque in the French pastry world, where he caught the world's attention with his Cherry on the Cake, a towering creation of hazelnut *dacquoise*, milk chocolate ganache, milk chocolate Chantilly cream, milk chocolate shavings, crushed wafers, and a bright red candied cherry—*phew!* complete with stem—on top. This was an important revelation for two reasons: its artistry and the unexpected flavors.

Unveiling this cake is a ritual, and if there's one thing I'd learned, it's that the French like their rituals. The more dramatic, the better. Untying the satin bow at the top of the cake's tall, triangular box allows the sides to fall away, revealing the gleaming cherry and six gold-leaf markings down the side, which indicate where to slice to serve the six perfect portions. With this cake, Pierre proved he was wildly creative, yet precise and thoughtful; a hedonist, but a hedonist with a little restraint and a lot of skill.

Just as with its design, the flavor of the Cherry on the Cake left the French gasping. While they're typically dark and bittersweet chocolate devotees, this cake is all milk chocolate. Pierre took a risk that his budding fan base would fall for the milk chocolate and not think him sacrilegious for eschewing the dark. Same thing with flavors like lychee, rose, and salted caramel, which are common these days, but were out there when Pierre introduced them to his macarons and cakes in the early days. People started noticing this young pastry chef and what he was doing with flavors and textures. And because his creations were so delicious, they started wanting more.

Pierre Hermé then launched Ladurée's Champs-Élysées location—essentially rounding out his CV with the most important names in the French pastry world—and finally journeyed to Japan to open his first eponymous pâtisserie in 1998. It wasn't for another three years that Parisians were treated to their own Pierre Hermé boutique. Now there are half a dozen locations in Paris, two in London, and seven in Japan, plus a dozen cookbooks and a line of tea, jams, and scented candles. *Oh, Pierre…*

———— ✳ ————

As all the other women rushed home to make dinner for two, I would be lusting after Pierre Hermé's gorgeous cakes, which seemed to be the one thing in the city that came in *individuel* sizes. They were impressive examples of both style and substance that reminded me of the fanciness of Lady M in New York. Back home, Lady M's signature Mille Crepes cake—twenty silky crepe layers that sandwiched vanilla custard and caramelized sugar—seduced me every time. But that seduction was like child's play in comparison.

At first, it was thrilling to scramble out of work so as not to miss the opportunity of having my love before the pâtisserie doors snapped shut for the night. Then, admittedly, it became a problem. Never mind how tight my agnès b. jeans had gotten; I realized the cakes and other sweets I was inhaling on a nearly daily basis were a substitute for the strong human embrace I really desired.

I knew from experience I'd have to wait in line at Pierre Hermé's sleek rue Bonaparte boutique, his original location, even in the evening. Indeed, there was a long queue on the sidewalk, and I suspiciously eyed the gray sky for raindrops as I joined it. Every few minutes, the snapping automatic doors would open and someone would exit. I would be a step closer to the rows of pristine cakes adorned with fresh berries, coffee beans, and dark chocolate shavings that waited inside—a step closer to cake heaven.

I breeched the entrance and inhaled deeply. The rich, intense scent of chocolate enveloped and comforted me. But the feeling of peace was short-lived. *Dear God*, I thought, scanning the amazing array of cakes before me, *somehow I have to decide what I'm going to order*. I eyed my options: the Saint-Honoré Ispahan, which looked like an elaborate Indian temple and was made with the same flavors that had previously made my knees tremble: rose macaron, rose Chantilly cream, lychee gelée, and topped with a fresh raspberry. Or maybe the Tarte Mogador, a spicy and smooth combination of short-crust pastry, milk chocolate and passion fruit ganache, concentrated pineapple, and a flourless chocolate biscuit. Dozens of options—and, by now, dozens of impossibly thin French women and lip-licking Japanese tourists behind me in line. My palms started sweating from the pressure. Then the elegant man on the other side of the counter looked squarely at me. "Mademoiselle?"

I was thrilled to be acknowledged as a girl instead of the "Madame" I had gotten used to, and my nerves calmed. I looked back down at the rows of resplendent cakes and it became plain as day. "Le Plenitude Individuel, s'il vous plaît."

Pierre debuted his Plenitude line in 2003. "Is it chocolate with caramel, or caramel with chocolate?" he teases, pointing out the contrasting, yet perfectly balanced chocolate and caramel pairing he uses in this line of macarons and cakes. Dark chocolate and salted caramel are flavors I know intimately. They never fail to make me happy.

I paid the hefty fee and took my petite dome-shaped cake filled with chocolate mousse, caramel, and *fleur de sel* to the Square des Missions Étrangères, a ten-minute walk toward the hoity-toity rue du Bac quartier. It's one of the few parks that has retained its quiet beauty instead of being built up with bright plastic playgrounds and screaming *enfants*. The perfect spot to sit on a quiet bench with my treasure.

I was loath to disrupt the many perfect squares of chocolate—all dark and glistening save for the one single white chocolate slab—that adorned the chocolate fondant. Staring at it, I realized another reason why I loved Pierre Hermé. It's not just that he made the most exquisite cakes in Paris or that he came up with the most mind-blowing flavor combinations. I was also instinctively drawn to him because he did things a little bit differently. He was a man not beholden to tradition and who blazed his own trail. In my own small way, I was doing the same thing. No matter how dreamy my life in Paris sounded, I had taken a risk moving there as a thirty-six-year-old. Falling in love with Paris had been easy. Living there was getting harder and harder.

I had told myself I would show a little restraint and not eat the entire cake. But there I was, staring at my last bite. *Oh well*, I rationalized, *at least it was only an* individuel *size.*

— ❋ —

I was terrified my third date in Paris was going to be another freak show; strike three and I would be out of the dating game altogether. Only two things gave me reason to hope otherwise. The first, my dear Melissa was setting me up. And second, she was setting me up with an American. At least there would be some sort of comfort and familiarity.

Indeed, the date was pretty good. It ended with a heavy

make-out session (ten times better than with the Swedish beanpole, which isn't saying much, but still...) and an exchange of numbers (unlike with Salt-and-Pepper, put to use that night with a fleet of texts). It even led to a second date in which a homemade chocolate praline cake figured prominently. Maybe he wasn't my tarte-tatin-making pastry chef. He definitely wasn't Pierre Hermé. But at least it wasn't a strikeout. There was hope for me yet.

MORE
Sweet Spots
ON THE
MAP

C'est vrai. Pierre Hermé is a rock star. A god. Every sweet freak should genuflect at his altar. But that's not to say there aren't a gazillion other amazing pâtissiers in Paris. If it's gorgeous gâteaux *you're after, prepare to become* une leche-vitrine *("window licker") at any of these places: La Pâtisserie des Rêves (in the 7e and 16e), Gérard Mulot (3e and 6e), Stohrer (2e), and Hugo et Victor (7e and 1er).*

Cake in New York tends to be more "cute" than drop-dead gorgeous. But that's okay; cute still tastes delicious in the hands of the right bakers. See for yourself at Amy's Bread (in Hell's Kitchen, the Chelsea Market, and West Village), Baked (Red Hook, Brooklyn), and Black Hound Bakery (East Village).

— [C H A P T E R 8] —

A GOOD CHOCOLATE CHIP COOKIE IS HARD TO FIND

*I*f April is the cruelest month then T. S. Eliot wasn't acquainted with Paris in November. Beyond the bad dates, bogus work environment, and all my botched but earnest attempts at being a walking, talking Parisienne, by year's end I just wanted to curl up in an air-mail box and go home to New York.

By that point, I figured, it was where I belonged. I was still struggling with the language and couldn't crack the social protocol. I could never tell if I should remain on *vouvoyer* terms with people or if I had broken through to the friendlier *tutoyer*. I was confused by the air-kiss greeting: should I make accompanying kissing sounds or just bump cheekbones? And every time I met a local and we talked about getting together, nothing transpired. Everyone told me the French were hard to infiltrate. But it's different when people talk about it as a concept, and when you actually experience the chill of their sangfroid every day.

Everything in this foreign city had an extra layer of difficulty. No matter what the task at hand, it required exceptional flexibility and demanded infinite wells of patience. When I asked about the status of the Ogilvy business cards I had ordered months ago, for example, the office manager told me, "Next week." For the eighth week in a row. My tree house's two-in-one oven-microwave started emitting a scary piercing sound that made use impossible and, instead of replacing it *tout de suite*, my jolly landlord told me to "have fun" with my first appliance purchase in France. Though a check I had deposited to my French bank account had cleared my U.S. account three weeks earlier, the money wasn't showing up and my bank rep wasn't responding to my email inquiries or phone messages, leaving me scrounging for lunch money and stewing in my juices. And I was feeling a little freaked out since my doctor had left a voice mail to go over some test results I'd had a couple weeks earlier. When I called back, however, she had left for a two-week vacation. While I was hoping the results were A-OK, my attention turned to Milo who had started crazily yanking out big tufts of fur from his haunches, requiring a whole new vocabulary for the vet that I didn't even want to know.

I suddenly understood what it was like to be handicapped, for I had become a mute. The simplest things rendered me a withering mess. I was clumsy and tongue-tied, intimidated and frustrated. Since I was alone so often (if you don't count Milo and his new bald patches), these dark thoughts and self-doubts just swirled around my head, leaving me with way too much time to dissect the crazy French and their crazy ways. Then I started wondering if it was just me. I started asking myself, "Am *I* crazy?!" and when I realized that I was talking to myself I thought, actually, *oui*, maybe I am! A crazy cat lady. My biggest fear, finally realized in the most spectacular city on earth.

It was all too much. I became so worn down and defeated by my ineptness that I started putting off every little action. The most mundane errand, like buying shampoo at the grocery store, was like a brainteaser, and I needed epic courage and concentration to call and make a dinner reservation. Everything required Herculean effort. As a result, I did nothing. There were bills to pay, appointments to schedule, and an avalanche of emails to catch up on. Then there was stuff like, you know, trying to figure out who to call at the Vélib' office to find out what the mysterious $57 charge on my credit card was all about. But I just couldn't be bothered. There was no time. It took too much energy. There were episodes of *Mad Men* to be downloaded and Jean-Paul Hévin *mendiants*— little chocolate disks adorned with nuts and dried fruit—to be annihilated. I knew this self-defeating behavior was only hurting me, but after all those months struggling as an outsider and feeling branded as a foreigner, I was also tired of being a tough cookie. Thank goodness I finally had a few friends to lean on.

——— ✸ ———

"So, it's going really well, huh?" I was talking to Jo about her blossoming romance, but it might as well have been Melissa since I'd had this same exact conversation with her just the day before. How was it that my two single girlfriends in Paris, my *only* girlfriends in Paris, had both recently started dating Frenchies? And both relationships, in true Gallic style, had quickly evolved into serious territory. There's no such thing as casual dating in France; you're either together or not. "You're really into him?" I asked with a smile that I hoped masked my anxiety.

As an Aussie, Jo relished the idea of scrambled eggs and strong coffee as much as I did, so we were also official brunch buddies. And lucky for us, Parisians were having a full-blown love affair with *le brunch*. But while most cafés and bistros offered overpriced prix-fixe menus of *viennoiserie*, *tartines*, eggs, bacon, fruit salad, green salad, coffee, and juice, in portions that incited locals to show shocking and unusual displays of gluttony, Jo and I sought out more modest places where we could indulge in à la carte Anglo dishes. Granola paired with tart Greek yogurt and fluffy blueberry pancakes were recent triumphs. Today, we had discovered Eggs & Co., a two-story sliver of a restaurant with crooked floors and low ceilings in one of Saint-Germain's hidden alleys that was all eggs, all the time. Jo had ordered *une cocotte*, a small dish of baked eggs, with ratatouille. I had scrambled eggs with smoked salmon coming my way. I didn't know why we called smoked salmon "lox" back in New York, what the difference was, or why I had never really eaten it before. But smoked salmon had become one of my favorite things in Paris.

"You know, it's going surprisingly well," Jo said with a blush. "I mean, I just didn't see this coming. And it's so easy. This is the first guy I've dated here who I really feel like I can be myself around. And he's really into me!" Then she laughed, surprised by her own proclamation. Ever the modest one, she quickly added, "Well, you know what I mean—he *seems* like he's into me."

"I'm sure he is! It certainly seems like he is. I mean, you guys spend so much time together. The chemistry's good, you have fun, you can communicate despite the language and cultural barriers...I mean, those are no small things!" Never the kind of girl to be jealous of my friends' relationships, I wanted Jo to understand that I was happy for her. In the past few weeks, I had already gone through the awkward and nervous early stages of a relationship with her: wondering if he'd call after they had met, debating the protocol of going Dutch in Paris, anticipating how the sex with a Frenchman would be. I was with her 100 percent. But I was also, maybe, over-enthusing just a little bit to conceal my own vulnerability.

Oh hell, who was I kidding? I was secretly annoyed. Seriously! I had finally made a couple good girlfriends in Paris—cool, single girls—and they both had to go and meet men the very same week. Now they were both smitten, locked in time-consuming relationships. And while I did love eating eggs with Jo, I couldn't help lamenting the fact that, with her in a relationship, we would no longer be trolling bars for men together.

It was another reminder that I needed to land my own man. Even my promising American with a penchant for baking had flamed out after he got simultaneously too clingy and too ranty, going off about the evils of advertising even though he knew it was what I did for a living. It was more righteousness, and a few too many lectures, than I could stomach so I called it quits.

Because I was spending so much time alone, I got pretty good at solo activities. I passed entire weekends by myself, Vélib'ing to pâtisseries, strolling through the open-air markets, and taking early morning walks along the Seine, especially on Sundays when the main road was closed to cars. I also took a slew of cooking classes, learning to make sole meunière and Provençal sardines, lavender *crème brûlée* and plum clafoutis, celery root soup and vegetable napoleons. It was all lovely and delicious. But what I really needed now was a girls' night out.

"So, what are you doing later?" I asked after our plates had been cleared and her relationship dissected. "Do you want to go to Chez Jeanette for some drinks?" I was thinking the allure of this newly discovered hipster bar on the seedy rue du Faubourg-Saint-Denis might tempt her.

"Ohhhh…" Jo squirmed a little. "Actually, I'm meeting Cedric's parents tonight. We're doing dinner." As I plied her with questions about this important new phase—meeting mom and dad just weeks into the relationship, *sheesh!*—I was mentally rifling through my alternatives. Michael was traveling to some exotic Eastern European capital that was known to have hot chicks. Melissa was with her new beau. Again. And, though by now I had a couple other acquaintances, I just couldn't picture texting them for a Saturday girls' night out. So I masochistically started going through my New York Rolodex, imagining what all my friends would be doing at about eight o'clock on a Saturday night. AJ and Mitchell would be cozied up over a romantic dinner, planning the rest of their lives together. Jonathan would probably be chatting up some sexpot at a loud, thumping gay bar. And I bet Mary, Melanie, Krista, and Carrie were getting all dolled up, ready to take on New York's latest hot spot. Oh, how I suddenly wished it were September again, when I was back home. I had wasted so much time pining for Paris when I was in New York. I hadn't stopped to appreciate all the creature comforts and the camaraderie surrounding me—how natural and easy things were.

But that was then, this was now. Now I was in Paris. City of romance. City of my dreams. And suddenly, a city where I knew no singletons. I almost cajoled Jo into ditching the parents and having some fun *avec moi*. But I knew that wasn't fair. She was in that lovely state of infatuation when everything was fresh and anything was possible. She deserved to bask in it. *Face it, Aim,* I told myself, *it looks like another Saturday night, just you and Milo.* Out loud, I tried to sound a little less pathetic and a lot more gracious.

"That's great, Jo. I'm so happy for you."

—— ✳ ——

When I first arrived in Paris, I was certain I was living some Cinderella story in which fairy godmothers materialized from bubbles to make my dreams come true. And with the highfalutin fashion, glamorous Champs-Élysées offices, and adorable tree house in the middle of the most delicious city in the world, why *wouldn't* I believe a little magic was at play? All that was missing was my tarte tatin prince!

After my initial giddiness when strolling through the Louis Vuitton flagship—pawing the silky gowns and spiky stilettos made me wonder why *I* was the lucky girl who got to live this dream—I was still asking questions as to just why I was there, but now instead of in a starry-eyed, I'm-the-luckiest-girl-in-the-world sort of way, it was a desperate, WTF sort of way. I thought things would get easier the longer I was in Paris.

But they just kept getting harder. Not even after my parents' divorce or breaking up with Max had I felt so alone.

In New York, with my packed social calendar, I had a rock-solid sense of self. Now that I had been on my own in Paris for months, I was increasingly tormented by my age and single status. Everywhere I looked, lovers were cuddling, cooing, and unabashedly making out. I kept hearing a taunting refrain, echoing louder and louder in my head: *Et moi? Et moi?* I started waking up in the middle of the night, questioning my decisions: why had I left Max in San Francisco all those years ago? Why did I never truly give Eric a chance? I was now wondering—perhaps a little late—about the repercussions. Why *didn't* I have a boyfriend? I couldn't help but feel negative. Adrift. I was a thirty-six-year-old American woman living in France. What the hell was I doing? What did I want? What was I searching for? If my dream was to live in the City of Light and Dark Chocolate, how come I was beginning to spend more and more time fantasizing about New York?

— ✳ —

I stopped at the Eric Kayser on rue Montorgueil for a chocolate chip cookie after brunching with Jo. If I was going to be spending quality time with *Mad Men* and Milo later that night, I reckoned, I might as well have a sweet to go with the show. It was more self-defeating behavior, going straight to my ass, but I didn't care. I needed it.

Chocolate chip cookies have always held a special place for me. But then again, what honorable American doesn't have a special softness for these classic baked goods that were the result of an accident? *An accident!* Imagine if Ruth Wakefield, owner of the Toll House Inn in Whitman, Massachusetts, circa 1930, had never knocked the Nestlé chocolate bar into her industrial mixer, as folklore has her doing? Would someone else eventually have had the brilliant idea of adding rich chocolate chunks to smooth and creamy cookie dough? Or would the chocolate chip cookie never have existed? I shudder to think not.

Interestingly, the tarte tatin, which is almost as iconic to the French as chocolate chip cookies are to Americans, was similarly said to be the result of a merry mistake. Caroline and Stéphanie Tatin were two sisters, coincidentally also running a hotel. After forgetting to place a crust along the bottom of a baking pan, Stephanie tried salvaging the dessert by draping a sheet of dough *over* her caramelized apple filling. Then, by inverting the creation after it had baked in the oven, *voilà*, the lovely and amazing "upside down" tarte tatin was presented to the world. But that's another story…

Growing up, it was a rare treat to bake Toll House chocolate chip cookies from scratch. We were a boxed-mix household. I mean, who had something as exotic as *vanilla extract* in the cupboard? Homemade cookies were a luxury.

When I lived in San Francisco in my twenties, I decided

I deserved to be treated every so often. I started the habit of renting two movies every Tuesday night and baking batches of Toll House ready-made dough. By then, I was accustomed to having vanilla extract on hand, but I was also lazier and more inclined to just get to the good stuff. The movies were dinner, the cookies were dessert, and my appreciation for and devotion to chocolate chip cookies—along with Martin Scorsese and Luc Besson—deepened each week.

By the time I moved to New York in 2001, I had moved beyond Toll House and was nothing short of a chocolate chip cookie snob. I knew there were many forms of magic at play in the making of the perfect chocolate chip cookie. It wasn't just a bowl of flour and sugar and eggs and chocolate chips that, when baked for eight to ten minutes at 350 degrees, created an afternoon snack (or Tuesday night dinner). There was serious technique, arrived at after studious experimentation. Letting the dough rest in the refrigerator anywhere from twelve to thirty-six hours, for example, lets the individual ingredients meld together, resulting in better baking consistency—a hydration tactic relied upon by practically every good baker. The scoop size of the raw dough going into the oven is also important, determining the crisp-to-chewy-to-melty ratio as one nibbles their way from the cookie's firm edge to its gooey, doughy center. Passion, imagination, quality—they're all just as important as they get artfully mixed in with the other ingredients.

While there were no cookie wars in New York the way there were for cupcakes, there were plenty of philosophies about the perfect chocolate chip cookie. Should it be soft or crisp? Fat or flat? Big or small? Austere or experimental? Different tastes and opinions propelled a healthy debate— and a delicious excuse to continuously sample all the specimens. And like everything else in New York, I discovered, the options just kept getting bigger, richer, and more outrageous.

———— ✳ ————

My New York chocolate chip explorations began with City Bakery, which was started in 1990 by Maury Rubin as a modest spot peddling savory food from one six-foot-long table and pastries from another six-foot-long table. Within ten years, Maury had not only catapulted to success, upgrading to a cavernous two-level cafeteria-style space in the Flatiron District, but City Bakery had become a city institution. Maury, a Parisian-trained baker himself, initially focused on tarts, *viennoiserie*, and other French specialties. But soon his American sensibilities muscled their way in. He introduced cookies to the City Bakery menu—lovely, dreamy, crunchy, creamy, soft, and sugary chocolate chip cookies. His saucer-sized beauties have it all: crispy edges, melty middles, and a buttery-gritty texture that's balanced by giant hunks of smooth dark chocolate. They have just a hint of caramel flavor. They're real cookie monsters.

Naturally I was smitten with City Bakery's cookies. But then Julie, who lived on the Upper West Side, introduced me to Levain, a subterranean hole-in-the-wall, and my loyalties were suddenly divided. This sublime little bakery was the result of two ambitious women who were hungry for a big challenge—and an even bigger cookie. Pam Weekes and Connie McDonald were training for the Ironman Triathlon in 1994. As a result of their rigorous swimming, cycling, and running training, the two friends were constantly famished, and the regular-sized cookies they found everywhere just weren't cutting it. So they baked up their own batches. And, after both successfully completed the triathlon, they opened Levain in 1995.

When Julie first took me there, she suggested that we split a cookie. Seriously? *Split* a cookie? What did she take me for, a weight-conscious waif who was intimidated by creamed butter and sugar? But once I saw the six-ounce whoppers being pulled from the oven and cooling on the racks behind the bakery's small counter, I understood. If City Bakery had cookie monsters, Levain's cookies were on steroids.

I consented to go halfsies with Julie, but only if we split *two* cookies. She might be the one with a ballet dancer's body, but I had the more logical mind. I told her to surprise me with her two favorites while I ran outside to snag the bakery's lone bench that was auspiciously being vacated at that moment by a khaki-clad dad and his chocolate-smeared daughter. I wondered which of the four flavors Julie would opt for: chocolate chip with roasted walnuts, dark and decadent chocolate chocolate chip, wholesome oatmeal raisin, or dark chocolate with peanut butter chips. A moment later, Julie came out toting a small but heavy paper bag. I peeked inside, and the revelation couldn't have made me happier: one chocolate chip walnut cookie and one double chocolate chip cookie. "Well done, *mon amie*," I commended, swallowing in anticipation.

I let her drive. Julie withdrew the chocolate chip cookie with walnuts, doing just as you're supposed to with a cheese platter and starting with the mildest and working your way to the richest flavor. She broke the little mound of cakey, chocolate-studded, slightly undercooked heaven in two and handed me half. "One, two, three!" she commanded. We bit in simultaneously and broke out into big, sexy smiles. Semisweet chocolate morsels smeared our teeth. Our eyes rolled in the back of our heads, our feet giddily tapping the sidewalk. "No way!" was all I could say. Julie, eyes closed, couldn't even respond. We were lost in cookie heaven.

And then it happened again. Perfectly happy to have City Bakery and Levain dueling it out for top chocolate chip cookie honors, I was ambushed in my own backyard in 2008. David Chang, who had become the darling of the New York restaurant world, thanks to his Momofuku noodle and ssäm bars in the East Village, opened his third outpost, Momofuku Milk Bar, just around the corner from my apartment. While everyone in the city was clamoring for the restaurants' bowls of brisket ramen and platters of pig butt, his pastry chef, Christina Tosi, was cooking up "crack pie," an insane and outrageously addictive concoction made largely of white sugar, brown sugar, and powdered sugar, with egg yolks, heavy cream, and lots of butter, all baked in an oat cookie crust. People were going nuts for the stuff, and it was time for me to give this crack pie a shot. But as soon as I walked into the industrial-style bakery, I knew crack could have nothing on the cookies.

Blueberry and cream. Double chocolate. Peanut butter. Corn. (Yes, a *corn cookie*, and it was delicious). There was a giant compost cookie, chock-full of pretzels, chips, coffee grounds, butterscotch, oats, and chocolate chips. But the real knockout was the cornflake, marshmallow, and chocolate chip cookie. It was sticky, chewy, and crunchy at once, sweet and chocolaty, the ever-important bottom side rimmed in caramelized beauty. I love rice crisps in my chocolate, but who would have thought that cornflakes in my cookies could also cause such rapture?

It was clear. New York offered every conceivable kind of chocolate chip cookie, from the rich to the ridiculous. But I had trouble finding a worthy contender in Paris. Until Eric Kayser.

—— ✳ ——

Eric Kayser's story is a classic French *boulanger*'s tale. The son, grandson, and great-grandson of Alsatian bakers, he knew from the time he was four years old that he too wanted to spend his life mixing batter and operating ovens. As soon as he was old enough, he started apprenticing with some of the country's best *boulanger*s and then went on to teach at France's national bakery school, l'Institut National de la Boulangerie Pâtisserie (INBP). After helping a number of other bakers launch their own businesses, it was finally time for him to open shop. In 1996, Eric Kayser debuted on rue Monge in the fifth arrondissement.

Kayser has always been, first and foremost, a bread maker, using carefully selected flours—whole wheat, buckwheat, rye, rough flax—and natural leavens that give his loaves, in all their infinite varieties, tender centers, golden crackly crusts, and beautiful complex flavors. But, as Mom, Bob, and I had discovered all those months ago (and I had confirmed on many subsequent visits to his rue Montorgueil *boulangerie*), his *douceurs* are also delicious.

Just as all the great chocolate chip cookie bakers in New York had experimented to come up with their perfect concoction, Kayser and his team of pastry chefs invested years in finessing the consummate cookie. Kayser traveled to the United States, searching for recipes he liked, and then adapting them for the French palette. The flour in France isn't as strong as in the U.S., for example, so that had to be altered. They also fiddled with how long the dough should rest in the refrigerator, fussed with the temperature of the oven, trialed and erred about how long the cookies should bake for, and played with the cookies' size.

"In the U.S., they make big cookies," he pointed out as if I weren't intimately familiar with cookies that dwarfed my palm and could build my biceps as I brought them to my mouth, bite after euphoric bite. "And sometimes in the U.S., they don't bake them enough." Which is true. But while some people like a crisp and crunchy chocolate chip cookie, I like mine the way Levain makes them: hulking and doughy, and flirting with rawness in the middle.

That's the wonderful thing about the chocolate chip cookie: there are infinite possibilities. And after years of kitchen wizardry, Eric Kayser also had his winner for the fussy French palette: *le cookie au chocolat*, made with Valrhona chocolate and toasted pecans.

— ✳ —

I now watched the woman place my *cookie au chocolat* on a sheet of thin bakery paper, fold it, and then twist the corners shut by working her hands in a rolling circular motion. I felt momentarily soothed by that lovely little French custom— almost as much as knowing that I'd soon have an American cookie in hand.

I carefully squirreled the cookie away in my bag and walked out into the narrow pedestrian streets, rue Montorgueil's markets and cafés especially animated now that it was late on a Saturday afternoon. That pang of longing in my belly I used to experience in my early days at seeing such bustling good cheer gave a little kick, reminding me that I was thousands of miles from home.

After climbing the six flights of stairs up to my Parisian tree house and saying hello to Milo, I stood before one of the arched windows looking out, wondering what to do. I used to love having no plans on a Saturday night. It used to be the biggest luxury, eschewing New York's crazy nightlife scene for some solo time with Netflix and the couch. Now it just felt sad.

Across the street, a woman in an apron was busy in her kitchen. From her open window, I could hear the sounds of running water, cupboard doors being slammed shut, and bowls and pans clanging against the countertops—inviting sounds of a happy home. Up above, the sky was gray. Across the horizon, the zinc roofs were gray. All around me, the limestone façades were gray. I had been telling myself a lot lately that these Parisian shades of gray weren't depressing. But I wasn't convinced. I was depressed.

No time like the present, I taunted myself, reaching for the cookie inside my bag, even though it was supposed to be for later.

I unraveled the paper, exposing my treat, and took a bigger bite out of it than necessary. The foreign but familiar flavors filled my mouth. I thought it strange how Eric Kayser's cookie had looked like it was going to be quite crunchy but was actually soft and chewy. And the giant rectangular chunks of chocolate that erupted against the cookie's surface had set me up for an über-rich experience but, in fact, it was tame. It wasn't like any of the chocolate chip cookies back home. But that was the point, right? There was no sense clinging to my American comforts and beliefs while living in Paris. No matter how much I tried, I wasn't going to replicate my friends back home or recreate my easy New York life.

I had come to Paris for a new chapter, I reminded myself. For new experiences and friends. For new tastes and possibilities. For a whole new way of learning —about the world and myself. I just hadn't expected that part of the "new me" would feel so forlorn that even a chocolate chip cookie would fail to make me smile.

MORE
Sweet Spots
ON THE
MAP

Like I said, New York is out of control when it comes to chocolate chip cookies. City Bakery, Levain, and Momofuku are my top three. (Maury, as much a hippie as a Francophile, opened several City Bakery offshoots called Birdbath, where all the fixtures are recycled and green, the ingredients are local and organic, and the cookies are still giant and delicious). Ruby et Violette is an Oprah-endorsed, closet-sized outpost in Hell's Kitchen with over one hundred crazy flavors (only about twenty are served at any one time) like root beer float, peach cobbler, or French vanilla. And not only does Jacques Torres make a mean cup of cocoa, his chocolate chunk cookies are killer—especially when you ask for one from the warming griddle, making it warm and gooey as if it just came out of the oven. Oink, oink!

There are just too many exquisitely perfect French delicacies to worry your American self about a chocolate chip cookie in Paris. But if you really, really need a fix, Fabrice Le Bourdat's Blé Sucré in the 12e and Laura Todd at Les Halles have commendable versions, and you can special order large and cakey, chocolate studded, golden-brown chocolate chip cookies by the dozen from Lola's.

CHAPTER 9

THE ECSTASY OF MADELEINES AND MUFFINS

*E*very day you wake up with a choice: will today be a good day or a crummy day? Am I going to complain about the stubborn rain and cloying cold, the lack of sexy options hanging in my closet, and the extra five pounds that are stuck to my ass? That I have to get dressed and go to work despite the weather, my wardrobe, and big ass? Or am I going to be grateful? Am I going to focus on how lucky I am to *have* a job, that I have legs strong enough to carry me to work, and that I have a family who loves and supports me, expanding ass and all?

I'm not saying you can't be in a bad mood or have bad days. Lord knows, I have my share. I'm a Scorpio, after all. If you don't believe in astrology, all you have to do is ask one of my friends if "moody" and "mercurial" are apt descriptions of my personality or ask one of my cousins—bless their hearts—which one of us our grandmother called "sourpuss" (hint: it wasn't any of them). But bad moods are exhausting. And if I learned anything in that long, dark winter in Paris it's that sometimes if you change your attitude, life follows your lead.

—— ❋ ——

One of my greater feats in Paris was finding an English-speaking GP who doubled as a gynecologist. Faking my way through transactions at the dry-cleaner or post office was one thing. But smiling with faux understanding, feet in cold metal stirrups, paper gown opened to reveal my whole front side, was just beyond my comfort and acting skills. Dr. Tippy was an English girl's secret weapon in Paris, the referral generously passed on to me from Jo when I finally decided to address some "female issues" I was having.

"So then, how're you doing?" Dr. Tippy asked in her clipped British accent. She was a fast talker. Even in the same tongue, I had a hard time catching just what the hell she was saying sometimes. And I wanted to be sure I heard every word she said today. It had been a good eight months since I'd had my period, and a couple weeks since I had come in for an exam and blood work. I wanted to know what was going on with my system. "Right, so I have the results to your blood tests," she barreled on, rifling through the papers on her big wooden desk, not waiting for my response. "Hmmm,

hmmm, that's right," she muttered to herself. I told the butterflies in my stomach to quit it, that everything was going
to be okay.

She finally looked up at me through her large owl glasses.
"It looks like your estrogen levels are really quite low," her
voice also starting to get low. My butterflies were now fluttering in a tizzy, Dr. Tippy's conspiratorial tone making me
nervous. It reminded me of that scene from *St. Elmo's Fire*
when everyone's gathered at the dining room table and the
mom whispers "cancer" because it's too ugly a word to say out
loud. Oh God, was that where our conversation was head-
ing? Were my nonexistent periods—something I had obviously known wasn't right but was one less thing I had to deal
with these past trying months—something more serious?
More ominous? Dr. Tippy was glancing back down at her
papers, voice now so low, she was purring. "They're almost
nonexistent, actually."

She continued talking, throwing out the names of female
hormones—LH, FSH, progesterone—but I could barely hear
her above the shrieking inside my head. *What the fuck? What
the FUCK?* This was all my fault. I knew I had ovarian cysts
when I came to Paris. My super high-tech New York gyno
had pointed them out to me on the sonogram screen and
told me the first point of action in treating this "polycystic
ovary syndrome" was going on the pill. That was three days
before flying off to a new life in Paris. I had shoes and books

to pack. People and bakeries to say good-bye to. Getting a birth control prescription just wasn't at the top of my priority list. So I, well, I sort of pretended she never said it. I knew it was foolish and immature, and the knowledge of those little cysts had been lurking in the back of my mind ever since. But my Manhattan doctor had also said the cysts were benign, quite treatable, and nothing to get alarmed about, so I didn't. Get alarmed. Until now.

"So, what does that mean exactly?" I asked, in a calm voice that I hoped didn't belie my internal profanity. "The 'nonexistent estrogen levels'?"

"Well, it could mean a few things," Dr. Tippy responded in her speed-whisper. As she started ticking these things off, the words she used, like "ovulation," "fertility," and "menopause," echoed nastily in my head. I felt rattled and disoriented. I didn't understand what was happening. And then it just got worse. "Do you have a partner?" she asked. "Are children something you're considering?" The benign look on Dr. Tippy's face gave absolutely no indication of how loaded her questions were. The room was unbearably quiet as she waited. Inconsolable babies wailed in the waiting room down the hall.

"No." *Was* I considering children? "I mean, yes." Exactly how *did* I feel about having kids? "No, yes. I don't have a partner right now, but I probably do want kids. I think. Some day."

"Well listen, you have time. You're thirty-six—oh wait, thirty-seven—I see you recently had a birthday," her reference a little twist to the dagger she had dug into my gut five minutes ago. "Well, no matter. But this is obviously something that needs to be addressed sooner rather than later, especially if you do think kids are something you want in your future."

Dr. Tippy briskly shuffled her papers again, this time with a determined spirit. "I can only do so much for you so I'm going to give you the name of an endocrinologist, which is a hormone specialist. She'll be able to explain things a bit further and take you through your options." She tore the referral from her prescription pad and gave me that doctor smile that's supposed to be calming and reassuring but just made me want to throw up.

— ✸ —

Needless to say, I was a wreck in the ensuing days. The littlest things—a conversational impasse at work, a rude Frenchie cutting me off in the street, my mom's photo on the fridge— were all it took to turn me into a geyser of salty tears. I had to wait two weeks before I could get in to see the endocrinologist, which left me, once again, with too much time inside my head. Alone with my thoughts. Doubting myself.

I kept hearing Dr. Tippy asking: *Are children something you're considering?* It was a good question—one that I had cleverly avoided for years. I had always thought that I first needed to meet someone who knocked my socks off. Someone I knew I wanted to spend the rest of my life with. Then, maybe then, I'd feel strongly enough about having kids. To me, starting a family was the result of loving someone so incredibly much that you wanted to make a baby with him. While I had been in love with Max and had lovely memories of Eric, I had been too young or our situations just weren't right for that sort of commitment.

Had I forever altered my life, being so heedless about my biological clock? Would those young and fertile, willfully ignorant, years come back to haunt me? While I still didn't necessarily know if I wanted babies, I certainly didn't want anyone telling me they weren't an option.

As I muddled through my angst, my instinct was to call one of my girlfriends back home, but I didn't feel right doing that. I didn't want anyone to feel guilty for their deserved good fortune. AJ's wedding was creeping up. She was getting married in a matter of weeks, and I knew she was excited to start trying to get pregnant. Everyone else already had kids, having largely gone the traditional route of marrying in their late twenties and starting families by their early thirties. I'd experienced a lot of the new motherhood drama with them: the lack of sleep, sex, and vacations. The soiled diapers, blouses, and couches. And the greater existential dilemmas like choosing between being a stay-at-home mom and a working mom, and the pressure to always be a super-mom. Listening to my friends struggle throughout the years, I had secretly considered myself fortunate that I didn't have to make those decisions. I knew it wasn't easy. And selfishly, I was psyched that I never had to sacrifice designer sofas, lazy Sunday mornings, or spontaneous sex.

I knew my girls wouldn't see it this way, but I felt if I called them now in a puddle of fertility woes, they'd feel guilty. I had always felt fulfilled and proud of my solo lifestyle—how it gave me freedom and made every day more fun, adventurous, and unexpected. This Parisian boondoggle was the perfect case in point. I could only do it because I was unattached and had no obligations except a monthly mortgage payment and Milo's cat food bills. And when I told everyone I was off to Paris to work on Louis Vuitton's advertising and learn the difference between choux pastry and puff pastry, they showered me with excitement and envy. "Take me with you!" they joked.

But now I was thirty-six years old—whoops, thirty-seven—and maybe the joke was on me. My knee-jerk "It would be nice if it happened" response had to be more carefully considered. I had been recklessly squelching the baby question, burying it deep inside of me as a maybe, maybe not scenario for years. Now it was maybe, maybe not too late. It was a reminder that I had stubbornly chosen to blaze a path of independence. The one on which I was now seemingly lost.

———— ✳ ————

"Oh, bunny, I'm so sorry. I know exactly what you're going through." As further evidence that Melissa and I were separated at birth, she really did know—five years earlier she had gone through a similar scare, hers leading to a final prognosis that she couldn't have kids. Now she was offering me the comfort and reassurance that I really needed at that moment.

"It's like my body is betraying me. I'm only thirty-six— damn, I keep doing that. I keep thinking I'm thirty-six. But I'm *thirty-seven*—"

"Still, Aim, thirty-seven is young. You have time."

"'Young' is pushing it. Thirty-seven is hardly 'young.' Especially when it comes to being a woman, much less getting pregnant." We looked at each other knowingly, the indignity of aging, and the injustice of getting older as a woman versus as a man, noted for a conversation another time. "But seriously, is this a sign of things to come? Am I just going to start decaying and falling apart? I mean, my ovaries just decided they were done with producing eggs?! And these cysts that I have? You know, sometimes you grow *beards* as a result!"

Melissa burst out laughing. "Beards?! What are you talking about?"

"It's true, it's one of the symptoms in severe cases!"

"I'm sorry, I shouldn't be laughing. This is serious. But I think the last thing you should be worrying about is a beard. There's nothing on your chin except adorable peach fuzz."

She reached out and cupped my face. I loved how affection-ate she was. We were sitting in her sun-filled living room that overlooked Canal Saint-Martin, sans makeup, sans pretense. As our friendship had developed over the months, an easy intimacy enveloped us that made hanging out at home as comfortable as if I were with one of my girls back home. We didn't need the distraction of a bustling bobo scene or the excuse of a new bar opening to get together. Listening to the bongos from the street urchins echoing across the waterway, seeing the chestnut trees swaying in the breeze outside her window, I was so grateful to have someone I could count on, heart and soul, in Paris.

"I don't think you're going to grow a beard, bunny. But I do think you're going to have kids. I just have a feeling that you're going to meet someone and be a mother. I really, really see that for you. I know it's not my lot in life, and I am fine with that, but I do think it'll happen for you."

"Really?" I asked imploringly, as if she were looking into a crystal ball and really could tell what my future held. I hadn't been able to figure it out all those years. Maybe Mel could.

"I know you have a referral—and, P.S., we don't even know what your situation is yet, this could just be a blip—but I can give you the name of one of the best fertility experts in the city, just so you have it."

I had so many questions and doubts, so much uncertainty and frustration about what was going on with my body.

Infertility? Babies? My future? *Mon dieu.* But having a friend to lean on made me feel invincible, if only fleetingly. The way a good AJ pep talk could. My appointment with the endocrinologist was tomorrow, and for the first time in two long weeks of waiting, I felt a sliver of optimism. I had Mel on my side. I could do this.

—— ✳ ——

I should have known better. By that time, I had been living in Paris for nearly nine months. I was intimately familiar with their all-business demeanor. Their eye-rolling and shoulder shrugging; their *meh* attitudes. So what did I expect, that this specialist I was sent to see would dispense hugs and compassion along with her prognosis?

There I was the next day, shivering in yet another gown, on yet another examination table, in a different part of town. Once again, I was subjected to a naked weigh-in and recital of my family's health history. My fingernails were blue, and my body was covered in goose bumps by the time we finally got to my current issues and symptoms. Despite my chills, my palms were collecting pools of sweat in my lap. I swallowed a lump of anxiety in my throat, but I managed to keep the tears in check. As I waited for the Specialist's expert opinion, I could get no read from her. I was dying. I felt like my whole biological future was in the hands of this heavy-set, beautifully coiffed, blank-faced endocrinologist.

"You know what you need to do?" she finally asked, her words coming like maddening drops in a bucket as opposed to Dr. Tippy's rat-a-tat machine gunfire. I shook my head and swallowed again. "Profiter d'être à Paris." She delivered this simple recommendation with complete and utter confidence.

"Eh, excusez-moi?"

"Profiter d'être à Paris," she looked at me and then repeated it yet again with more emphasis. "*Profiter d'être à Paris!*" Okay, where was the hidden camera? This was a joke, right? From what I understood, I was being treated for ovarian cysts and had iffy fertility prospects, and she was telling me to simply benefit from being in Paris? I wanted a hardcore plan of action. I wanted a course of treatment. I wanted drugs! After all, what could going to the theater and opera do for my ovaries?

If I were in New York, I knew I would be getting all kinds of prescriptions and advice. But the Specialist—in typical French fashion—shrugged the whole thing off. So, my internal stressing about living in a new country and culture has caused my system to go a little nutty? *C'est normal.* So my ovaries were temporarily withholding my eggs? *Pas grave.* So I was thirty-seven? *Peu import.* I just needed to relax.

The oral contraceptives Dr. Tippy had prescribed—and this time I was taking them—were meant to trick my system into "working" again and eventually make those cysts go away. I was still young and lively. Now, if I could just enjoy being there—see some Balanchine, eat some foie gras, do what so many people around the world would kill to do in my position—well, that would make me all better! I could have a healthy body and pump out some healthy babies. *Pourquoi pas? Why not?*

My feet limply dangled over the examination table as I waited for her real advice—a prescription, the name of another specialist, even some Eastern herbs or meditation techniques, anything tangible that I could walk away with to make me feel in control of the situation. But I was waiting for nothing. The Specialist rose from her desk, pushed a curl behind her ear, and wished me *bonne journée*.

As I pulled on my jeans—damn, *definitely* tighter than they used to be—exhaustion from these past couple weeks of emotional roller-coasting set in. A storm of feelings hit me at once: irritation, disbelief, fear, sadness, regret. And yet I found myself giggling. This long, drawn-out process capped off by the indifference of the Specialist was utterly absurd. And par for the course in Paris. *Vive la France!*

— ✳ —

I found myself wandering aimlessly through the twelfth arrondissement after my appointment, muttering to myself. That's it! Just enjoy being in Paris! Easy-breezy! No need to worry about your biological clock, mademoiselle—you might as well be *twenty-seven*!

But as I passed by the green awning of Blé Sucré, Fabrice Le Bourdat's pâtisserie on Square Trousseau, something clicked. If Marcel Proust, the French literary genius, had famously had an awakening biting into a plump little teacake known as the madeleine, maybe I could have a similarly transporting experience? If not an involuntary memory, perhaps an involuntary attitude adjustment? Fabrice's citrus-glazed madeleines were reputedly the best in the city. Could one of his special sponge cakes be the key to my moving forward? I knew I couldn't turn back the hands of time, but might something be triggered, releasing my pent-up hormones, flooding me with fertility, setting my body back in equilibrium? Could a madeleine make me better? If nothing else, I knew it would at least taste good. I went inside.

Considering Fabrice had been pâtissier at the five-star Bristol Hotel, which is known for its divine desserts, and, prior to that, the chic Plaza Athénée and Hotel de Martinez in Cannes, he has an extraordinarily calm and blasé perspective on baking (not unlike the Specialist's attitude had been about my ovaries). After the regal résumé building, he and his wife opened a modest bakery in 2006—the kind of neighborhood spot that everyone wants in their quartier. Every morning, and in waves throughout the day, lines stretch out the door, regulars waiting for his crunchy baguettes, flaky *viennoiserie*, and massive selection of *petits gâteaux*. Some, like the dome-shaped Le Vollon, are so glossy, the decadent dark chocolate looks molten. Others, like the L'Aligre, are as fluffy as clouds, topped with spears of candied pineapple. Fabrice's wife, Celine, cheerfully serves the customers, and then many mingle at the pastel-colored, iron café tables in front of the bakery. Sometimes Fabrice will join them for an espresso. Indeed, nothing makes the pâtissier happier than pleasing his customers—with his baking and his friendship. In return, many Parisians insist his baguettes and pain au chocolat are the best in the city. But nary a soul will dispute that his madeleines take top honors.

These shell-shaped teacakes from the town of Commercy in northeastern France date back to the eighteenth century. Made with *génoise* batter, which relies heavily on eggs, the edges bake to a dark golden color while the rest of the cake remains a sunny yellow. They can be put away in a quick five or six bites, making it nearly impossible to not reach for a second, and a third. They're sort of similar to American muffins—if you disregard the current super-sized, candy-studded bastardized muffins that have become so popular in recent years. Although there's at least one place in New York that has held onto the simple, wholesome concept of a muffin: Thé Adoré in Greenwich Village.

— ✳ —

Despite the French name, it's a Japanese gentleman by the name of Yukihito Yahagi who opened the two-story tearoom twenty years ago. A small crew of cute and fashionable Japanese women work there, churning out simple sandwiches, soups, and quiches. And they make fresh baked goods in the morning. True to a French salon de thé, they bake traditional pastries like almond croissants, brioche, and even madeleines. But they don't compare to the ones in Paris. While Fabrice's madeleines are moist, light, buttery, and delicious, Thé Adoré's are a titch on the dry, crumbly side—evidence that imitation may be the greatest form of flattery, but it's tough to beat a French pâtissier at his own game. And with Fabrice's thin layer of orange *glaçage*, made with freshly squeezed juice, he definitely has the winning touch.

Thé Adoré's muffins, however, are outstanding. Simple. Unpretentious. Lovely and delicious. Instead of softball-sized creations bursting with absurd mix-ins, there are only three varieties—raspberry, banana, and classic blueberry. They're baked in humble parchment paper, and are the same size that our moms ate in the '50s. They have a real do-it-yourself, made-at-home sensibility that I love.

It became a favorite escape of mine in New York: having morning coffee and a blueberry muffin—so classically American—but in a shabby-chic, French-Japanese tearoom. With dark wood tables and mismatched chairs scattered across the plank floors, the upstairs dining room felt as cozy as a cabin in the Catskills. Until you gazed out the giant picture window over 13th Street and saw all the NYU students rushing about with their yoga mats and shih tzus, and realized you were in the epicenter of New York. Still, I always found Thé Adoré romantic and peaceful. It's one of the few places in the city where you can sit with your thoughts and disappear for a while.

—— ✸ ——

And there I was, doing the same thing thousands of miles away. I had gotten a bag of four madeleines—the way they're sold at Blé Sucré—and retreated to Square Trousseau. The limestone apartment buildings stood guard over the neighborhood park, sunlight filtering through the bare chestnut trees. A big gazebo was smack in the middle of the park. Vacant ping-pong and foosball tables—*babyfoot* to the Frenchies—were lined up like soldiers on one side. The other side was consumed by a giant children's playground. As I looked around, I saw I wasn't the only one in the park indulging in a sweet.

Seeing as it was four o'clock in the afternoon, it was *le goûter*—the glorious hour when snacking was sanctioned. All the little rug rats were nibbling golden madeleines like mine, or *pain au chocolat*. A few humbly ate biscuits from the supermarket. But there were no fruit leathers or crackers powdered with orange "cheese." French kids learn early the importance of good food. The climbing walls and slides on the playground echoed with cute voices, and, every once in a while, was punctuated by not-so-cute screams and cries. A public park in Paris was hardly the place to come for a respite from thinking about kids.

Perhaps it was coincidence, or maybe madeleines—*good* madeleines—really do have transformative powers. All I can say is Fabrice's moist, citrusy teacakes were at least in part responsible for lifting me out of my funk. As I sat on a park bench, savoring the wee spongy snacks, my mojo started returning. Even if I didn't like the Specialist's advice, I couldn't complain. Someone was telling me to enjoy Paris. To take advantage of living in such a phenomenal place—which was the reason I had come to begin with. It's true, I realized, I *was* lucky. Lucky to be living in Paris, on my own path in life. I simply couldn't cry over yesteryears and what might have been.

I had spent thirty-seven years following my heart and my gut. There was no point in doubting myself now. When I had been younger and in relationships, it hadn't felt right to get married and have kids. And as shaky as I had been feeling lately, I knew I didn't regret those decisions. Maybe I'd still be so lucky to meet someone who knocked my socks off and have kids like Melissa predicted. Maybe I wouldn't. But, as the crumbs from my final madeleine disintegrated on my tongue, I knew that everything would work out the way it was supposed to. Bite by spongy-sweet bite, my emotions were being reset.

So I was willing to accept the Specialist's optimistic

prognosis. I decided 2010 was indeed going to be the year I profited by being in Paris. I had a belly full of pastries. The winter sun was warm and gentle. And it was a new day in Paris. It may have started out pretty crummy, but things were starting to get that golden glow again.

MORE *Sweet Spots* ON THE MAP

The current love affair between New York and Paris means you can get plenty of plump madeleines in New York, and multiflavored muffins in Paris. It may not be on the same scale as the cupcake-macaron exchange, but the Franglais sweet swap is becoming increasingly popular for these small, unsung douceurs as well.

In New York, you can get a nice, moist madeleine at Duane Park Pâtisserie in Tribeca, Ceci-Cela in Nolita, or at the ever-expanding Financier Pâtisserie chain. For muffins in Paris that will transport you to America, stop by Bob's Juice Bar in Canal Saint-Martin, Columbus Café in the Marais, or Lili's Brownies Café in Saint-Germain.

— [CHAPTER 10] —

CARROT CAKE IS THE NEW BANANA CAKE

*N*ow, I've…had…the time of my life…and I owe it all to yooooo-uuuuu…"

Ah, America. It was good to be back. JFK was as bustling as it always was. The *Dirty Dancing* soundtrack blaring from the speakers reminded me of the summer afternoons in high school I used to spend cruising around my Connecticut beach town in my little silver Jetta. Kim Kardashian and Lady Gaga blanketing every magazine cover reminded me how woefully out of touch I was with *le smut du jour*. Babies were screaming from their thousand-dollar strollers, cell phones were bleating like an electronic symphony, everyone—even barely walking three-year-olds—was tugging those little wheelie suitcases behind them, creating a candy-colored, movable minefield as I made my way from the Air France terminal to U.S. customs.

This was the same sensory overload that had appalled me when I made my first trip back home only a few months earlier. But now, surrounded by people sporting velour tracksuits, fake tans, and tattoos—such a long, long way from the slim jeans, ballet flats, and perfectly painted lips back in Paris—it was like a big, warm, chubby hug from America. This time, I wasn't complaining.

Maybe it was just the new outlook I had adopted since the Specialist: be happy and grateful for what you have, and watch how the world opens up to you. As proof that the universe was indeed trying to be more cooperative and supportive, the Louis Vuitton photo shoot I had to do for work had been scheduled in New York the week before AJ was getting married. I got to fly home for business and stay for my best friend's wedding. Not too shabby. Even better, we were booked at 60 Thompson, the slick boutique hotel in western Soho. Every morning I power-walked along the Hudson River Park, the narrow riverside stretch that extends from 59th Street to Battery Park and offers one of my favorite vantages of the city. In the evenings, we'd unwind in the lobby with cocktails, watching the parade of foreign guests toting their shopping bags filled with designer loot. Best of all, room service left a couple itty-bitty Fat Witch brownies on the nightstand every afternoon. I also wasn't above plundering the housekeeping carts, eschewing the Kiehl's bath products in favor of amassing a personal stockpile of fudgy two-bite treats. And "work" those few glorious days consisted of prepping for and then shooting Annie Leibovitz and Mikhail Baryshnikov—two artistic legends—for our latest campaign. *A girl can get used to this*, was the first thought that danced through my mind every morning when I got my sunny wake-up call from the front desk and flicked on NY1 to see what Pat Kiernan was reading in the papers.

But even though the workweek was decadent and exciting, it was also draining. When my team took off for the airport at the end of the jam-packed week, I heaved a happy sigh of relief and migrated uptown. I was home! In New York! My best friend was getting married, and we were going to have the time of our lives!

— ✳ —

"A, you look stunning!" Of course every bride looks beautiful, but AJ was truly radiant. And she wasn't even in her gown or makeup yet. It was the night before the wedding, and instead of having a traditional rehearsal dinner, AJ and Mitchell were hosting a casual open house in a Brooklyn Heights brownstone. It was the perfect representation of them as a couple: unfussy, fun, and all about home, family, and friends.

"Merci, mon amie," she replied, giving me an unguarded smile that made her blue eyes light up and her nose crinkle. It was like she couldn't contain her joy; this was the happiest I had ever seen her—even happier than when her braces came off in tenth grade. It was so crazy to think that when I had left New York not even a year ago, she and Mitchell had only just met. Now they were mere hours away from exchanging wedding vows. You never know what—or whom—life is going to bring you.

As the house filled up with guests, the energy progressed from relaxed to celebratory. It was a special occasion for me too—a chance to see so many people from years past and reminisce with my best friends from high school. Ben was about to sign a new band, Julie was convinced her daughter was going to be even naughtier at sixteen than she was now at four, and Elisa's husband was producing a new show on MTV. I caught up with AJ's aunts and uncles, most of whom I hadn't seen since I went to Iowa with AJ as a thirteen-year-old, severely obsessed with how high I could tease my bangs and just when I would have enough to fill out a training bra. Little cousins and children of friends, amped up on M&Ms, excitedly ran around the spacious parlor rooms; Van Morrison, Alicia Keys, and Coldplay shuffled on iTunes; and the buffet table was slowly being depleted of its cold cuts, crudités, and cupcakes.

At the end of the night, instead of rallying for a nightcap with the rest of the crew like we normally would have, AJ and I taxied back to Manhattan. She wisely wanted to get a good night's sleep. I was her Best Girl, there to ensure her wedding weekend worked out exactly as she wanted.

Besides, my feet were aching from standing all night in the new Charles Kammer lace-up heels I had bought in Paris for the wedding.

"How are *you* doing, Aim?" she asked once we were snuggled between the starchy sheets and down blankets on opposite sides of the king-sized bed of her bridal suite. AJ's compassion and sincerity had always—for lack of a less hokey term—warmed my heart. After these past few months of so little empathy or connection in my life, they were especially welcome. I was relieved to let my guard down.

"I'm good," I told her. "It's definitely been a rough couple of months, but I'm hanging in there." I listened to the taxi horns and police sirens echoing in the cavernous avenue twenty stories below, blessedly muted through the double-pane windows. A door slammed somewhere down the hall, another reveler's night coming to a close.

"I never even knew I could feel as depressed as I did last month in Paris," I continued. "I hit a new low. But, who knows? Maybe the ovarian cysts were the best thing to happen to me." AJ was looking at me quizzically, waiting for me. "It's been unsettling and…crappy," I went on. "And I really don't like thinking that there's a possibility I can't have kids. But at the same time, I also sort of feel like I've been given a second chance. I've had to really think about things—what my priorities are and what I want to achieve in my life—instead of just cruising along, you know? It's like a not-quite-midlife opportunity to decide what I want to do and where I want to go from here."

"It's so true, Amy. I mean, look at you," she paused for dramatic effect. "You're living abroad in the most beautiful city on earth. You work on Louis Vuitton's advertising. You're traveling every month. You're surrounded by all this great fashion, and fabulous people—"

"And don't forget the mind-blowing sweets!"

"Seriously. It's pretty amazing."

"I know, it is." I rolled on my back and gazed up at the ceiling, letting this moment of affirmation settle over me. I thought of the trips I'd taken in recent months—to London to spend time with my brother and his family, and to Nantes and Lille, two cities on opposite sides of the country that both had incredible art, architecture, and, *bien sûr*, sweets. I thought about how fulfilling my new friendships with Melissa, Michael, and Jo were, and also how much more I now valued the connection with my friends and family back home. I was also excited about the new community of bloggers I was becoming part of and even the fondness I had for my colleagues. I'd experienced the lowest lows and the highest highs of my life, those past months in Paris.

Thank God I had decided to slog through my loneliness and fear and not run home with my tail between my legs when things started getting hard. I had been ready to quit everything and go back to New York's comfort and familiarity. But by doing so, I would have walked away from the best career run I'd had in my life. I never would have seen so much of the French countryside. I wouldn't now eat duck, rabbit, herring and sardines, and about eighteen varieties of cheese and wine would be woefully unknown. Only weeks ago, I was convinced I belonged in New York. Now I felt I belonged in Paris.

While there were still questions—how long did I want to stay, where should I push my career, would I actually fall in love and have kids—I also knew that finding the answers required effort and patience. But finding those answers was why I was in Paris. "I mean, it sucks that I haven't met anyone and I still struggle with the language and meeting people," I continued my mini-therapy session with AJ, who was propped up on her elbow. I turned and mirrored her. "But everyone has their issues wherever they are. And I'm just trying to focus on the positive and believe that what's meant to be, will be." I paused. "And it will, I really believe that. Do I sound crazy new-agey?"

"Not at all. I think you have the right attitude. We never know what tomorrow will bring, so just enjoy your time in Paris, Aim. You're lucky to have the freedom to be doing what you're doing and enjoying so many cool things. You should be proud of yourself," she cheered me on. "It's not easy moving to a foreign city, where you know no one."

"Thanks, A," I said. "But enough about *moi*. This is it! You're getting *married* tomorrow. It's crazy, isn't it?"

"I know, married. It doesn't seem real." AJ got sucked into a mini-reverie, her eyes going glassy. Then she looked at me. "We've had so much fun."

"You and Mitchell?"

"No! You and me! Remember all the nights at Passerby?" she asked, referring to a tiny Chelsea bar with a flashing *Saturday Night Fever* dance floor. Inevitably, it was where we ended up during our single years, boogying until the wee morning hours.

"Yeah, and kir royales at Pastis…"

"And hanging out with Warren and Eddy at Bond Street…"

"Oh yeah, I had forgotten about them!" I confessed. After all, our nights had tended to be anchored far away from Noho in the circus-like Meatpacking District and dark, meandering streets of the West Village. "And remember the parties we'd throw at Craig's apartment? Those were *so* fun." We might as well have been talking about our sweet sixteens or senior prom with the amount of nostalgia we were dredging up.

AJ started laughing. "Remember how you did your demo of side crow in your purple party dress? Those pictures are *awesome*."

"Yeah, and then of course Craig has to upstage me by doing full crow into a flying headstand." We were both cracking up at the image of me and our good friend doing yoga moves at various cocktail parties throughout the years. Don't ask me why we did it, but we did. It happened once and then became a regular party trick. "And remember Giles? Remember that night we met him and Gino and went back to their apartment and were up all night, dancing to the Bee Gees?"

"My God. When was the last time you saw the sun come up?"

"Uh, that night," I shuddered. "I think it took me about a week to recover."

This was it: our last single girls' night together and instead of tearing up the town, we were giggling like schoolgirls, remembering all the previous nights in the city that we had made lifelong memories—and, on occasion, fools of ourselves. But at least we had gotten the most out of our time together in New York. Although I knew AJ and I would always be this close, I also knew we were saying good-bye: to our old lives, to a time when we were young and wild and free in New York City. With me in Paris and AJ going to the altar, we were officially entering a new phase, a time when banana cupcakes and late-night cocktails would be more occasional than *de rigueur*. Soon even a modest pleasure like sitting at Billy's would be a rare event.

"We've been so lucky," I said as our laughter died down.

"So lucky, I know." AJ and I looked at each other in a moment of shared history. I could see her as a gangly, eager-to-please seventh grader; a nervous college freshman with her yellow Chevrolet packed full of boxes; a star shimmier on the dance floor of Passerby. No matter what, we would always be soul sisters.

"Let's get some sleep," I suggested, reaching for the bedside light. "Tomorrow's kind of a big day, you know."

"You're right," AJ smiled. "Night, Aim."

"Good night. Love you."

"Love you too."

———— ✳ ————

Between getting my hair and makeup done and finding a strapless bra, to-the-knee slip, and sheer black stockings—things I had desperately needed for the wedding but were much less intimidating and stressful to shop for in New York than Paris—and also attempting to make it to Billy's to get AJ a wedding-day banana cupcake, I had to finish writing my toast. Despite a brief run on the junior high debate team, public speaking has never been my forte. In fact, I hate it. And even though this toast was for my best friend, the thought of standing beneath the soaring ceilings of the Yale Club's main banquet hall, where the eyes of 120 live guests plus the framed portraits of five Yale-educated U.S. presidents would be watching me try to be equal parts charming, funny, sincere, and eloquent, made me feel as nauseous as if I had "accidentally" devoured all 1,080 calories inside a pint of Ben and Jerry's Phish Food ice cream.

But writing the toast was cathartic too. Having started it

thirty-six hundred miles away gave me some literal distance to reflect on a near lifetime of friendship with AJ: the search for love in both of our lives, the romantic ideals and fantasies we had formed—and that had formed us along the way. Our notions of who the perfect partner was had changed over the years, from cool New England prepsters in our teens, to worldly and artistic charmers in our twenties, to just feeling lucky if we could meet someone sane and gainfully employed without children, a drinking problem, or latent misogynistic tendencies by the time we were in our midthirties.

While I had been one of those girls who had her brides-maids' and babies' names picked out at the age of eighteen, at thirty-seven my life clearly looked nothing like the one my younger self had envisioned. But sometimes you want things just because you think you're supposed to. And sometimes it's the things you never even knew you wanted that give your life the most meaning. At the very moment that AJ was diving into the dream life we had fantasized about growing up together, my heart had led me further afield. My heart had taken me to Paris.

———— ✳ ————

The Anglo-Franco mélange of two cultures that I was expe-riencing in my personal life could also be seen in the rising popularity of certain sweets around Paris. In fact, the English baker Rose Carrarini's individual carrot cakes—the shape and size of Campbell's soup cans, topped with a measured layer of cream cheese frosting—had become icons of *la cuisine anglaise* ever since she and her French husband, Jean-Charles, opened Rose Bakery in 2002 on the then little-trafficked rue des Martyrs in the ninth arrondissement.

Prior to that, the couple had already cooked up a successful food empire in London called Villandry. After growing and selling that business, they decided to venture south for a new chapter: a smaller bakery where they could be more hands-on.

It's sort of ironic that carrot cake came to symbolize their nouveau eatery as Rose didn't have formal pastry training, nor does she have a sweet tooth. But what she and Jean-Charles did have was a passion for healthy, organic ingredients, a keen sense for the next new thing, and some strong connections. Rose's sister-in-law is Rei Kawabuko, the designer behind Comme des Garçons, and they created half the menu for Colette, the hypercool concept store on rue Saint-Honoré that lured international hipsters with its selection of bespoke *baskets*, electronic music, and art-house books. Even though the couple was intentionally vague about where and when they would be opening their bakery, word got out and trendy Parisians were queuing before it even opened.

Just as the couple's intention was always to dissolve the distinction between home and restaurant cooking by offering simple, wholesome food, they also blurred the boundaries of the kitchen and dining room of their rue des Martyrs canteen. The dishes—vibrantly colored market salads, square-shaped quiches with organic veggies spearing the eggy surfaces, and rows of marble cake, citron polenta cake, pistachio cake, plus the cylindrical carrot cakes—were arranged on a short counter immediately to the right of the entrance. This gave customers—who stood hovering over the display as they inevitably had to wait for a table—a chance to peer at what might soon be in their bellies.

Rose's dalliances in sweets began back in London when she couldn't find pastries and desserts that she wanted to eat and decided she'd have to do it herself. As soon as she took on the challenge of making pastry dough at Villandry, she realized there are many factors that go into successful baking besides just following a recipe. How you handle the dough and when you take it out of the oven can affect the taste as much as the ingredients that you put into the mixing bowl. She'd touch her pastries until they felt the right consistency and taste them until they were perfect to her palate.

It wasn't just technique where Rose proved to be a natural. She was, and is, a genius recipe developer. She taught herself through practice, by listening and responding to customers' desires, by reading the likes of Elizabeth David and Richard Olney, and by drawing inspiration from great chefs such as Alice Waters. She started with classic recipes and then twisted them to see how she could transform each dessert into something different—something better. Letting her instincts lead the way, she kept playing with recipes, adjusting measurements and altering ingredients, which, more often than not, meant reducing the amount of sugar. For example, she cut the sugar in her now-famous carrot cake by half of what the original recipe called for. As a result, Rose's desserts are intentionally healthier than most. This philosophy is "the culmination of years of our taking out what is not necessary" is how she puts it in her delicious cookbook *Breakfast, Lunch, Tea*.

For the better part of a year, I had watched Anglo eateries popping up all over Paris. Just like on my visits to New York when I discovered new French bakeries, it brought me an uneasy mixture of excitement, pride, and serious annoyance. It was comforting to see familiar desserts, but it was jarring and bizarre too. After all, who wants to eat carrot cake when there are black currant macarons, raspberry-rose *millefeuilles*, and triple chocolate terrines studded with caramelized Piedmont hazelnuts? *Pas moi.* I was flummoxed as to how Parisians could be seduced by a totally unsexy dessert. But there it was: this humble cake of shredded root vegetables had made quite an impression on the Frenchies.

---- ✸ ----

"I think it goes to show you, some of the best things in life are worth waiting for." I was nearly done delivering my toast. My voice had stopped quivering halfway through, I was standing taller, with more confidence, and I think George W. even winked at me in empathy from his portrait on the banquet room's wall. "So everyone, please raise your glasses—here's to AJ and Mitchell!" After two minutes of sucking in my gut before all the guests, I exhaled. The MC plucked the microphone from my sweaty palm and I fled to the safety of my table for eight, where a ninth chair had been crammed in so I could sit with my four best coupled friends. With the toast behind me, it was time to party.

It was one of those weddings that starts with everyone looking coiffed and civilized but quickly spirals into a roiling sweat-fest. Mitchell had spent weeks putting together a playlist that married his passion for indie '80s music with AJ's devotion to disco. As evidenced by the packed dance floor, it appealed to AJ's still-spry grandma as much as all us "kids" from high school days. With each hour, more mascara was smeared, more updos came tumbling down, and more neckties were tossed on the now-empty dinner tables. There were blistered feet, torn pantyhose, and more than one air guitar battle. It was brilliant.

"Yeah, Paris!" I excitedly shouted to Tom, one of AJ's friends from her stint in Washington, D.C., whom I had bumped into while getting another glass of prosecco at the bar.

"Wow, that's pretty awesome."

"Yeah, I love it. It's amazing."

"I bet the food's incredible," Aunt Val said when we were both catching our breath after pogo-ing to Kris Kross.

"Oh-my-God-*in*-credible," I gushed. "I mean, it's like, how can *an apple* taste so delicious? Everything—the baguettes, the butter, the wine, the pastries—is just so flavorful, it's insane."

"How are the men?" two of AJ's college girlfriends wanted to know. We were in the restroom, trying to salvage our matte complexions but were resigning to the fact that a fresh application of lipstick was about as good as it was going to get. "Bahh…" I dramatically shrugged my shoulders and immediately recognized that—*sacré bleu!*—with that simultaneous utterance and shrug, I was mimicking a French mannerism that drove me crazy back in Paris! I shook my head at the question and myself. "Let's just say that I haven't exactly figured the men out."

Without a date that night, I was floating—free, happy, proud, and excited. I could flit about and talk to everyone. For the first time in a very long time—definitely the first time in Manhattan, city of searching for Mr. Right—I didn't care about being single. So I didn't have a fabulous plus-one at my side. I had a fabulous *life* back in Paris. I was enjoying how everyone responded to those two simple syllables when they fell from my lips: Pair-iss. They sighed, swooned, and became starry-eyed. Or maybe that was just how it made me feel.

---— ❋ —---

If a good wedding can be judged by how much your feet throb the next day, then AJ's wedding was a roaring success. As I stretched back in my seat on the flight back to Paris, achy, blistered feet released from the captivity of my leather boots, I was feeling downright giddy. It was everything and nothing: the dancing, the goofiness, the howling-in-laughter jokes, and the tender moments. The previous few days with my best friends in New York had given me the surge of love and reassurance I needed as I went back to Paris to embrace six more months of the unknown.

MORE
Sweet Spots
ON THE
MAP

Banana cake with cream cheese frosting is offered at many a New York bakery, from Baked to Sugar Sweet Sunshine to Amy's Bread. But, in honor of AJ, Billy's gets my seal of approval. Since opening in Chelsea, they've gone on to open additional outposts in Tribeca and Nolita.

By the end of my stint in Paris, there was a crazy wave of Anglo-American eateries that offered cheese-cake, pound cake, cupcakes, and carrot cake, including Merce and the Muse in the Marais, and Cosi and Lili's Brownies Café, both in Saint-Germain. But Rose Bakery is definitely the place for carrot cake. Just like Billy's, Rose and Jean-Charles have slowly expanded with outposts in the Marais and the Bastille. Could New York be next?

—[C H A P T E R 1 1]—

RESURRECTION COMES FROM BABA AU RHUM

As the language and cultural barriers began to feel ever so less foreign to me a year into my Parisian stint, another feeling emerged that was almost as disconcerting: Suddenly, I loved my job.

This was totally new to me. Sure, I've enjoyed my advertising career well enough. But it's mostly been the people and atmosphere that I've liked. I've had amazingly kind and talented creative directors (they do exist!), fun and collaborative art directors for partners, and I've made genuine and lasting friendships. Then, of course, there are the perks of being in a creative industry—things like boozy happy hours that yield salacious gossip; decadent client dinners at which you order way too many courses and bottles of wine because someone else is footing the bill; and platters of cookies left over in the conference room after meetings. But advertising never *moved* me. It was something I did to pay the bills (and my imported chocolate habit). Until now. With the Louis Vuitton relaunch project underway, I was doing some of the most exciting work of my career.

A lot had changed since my breakdown six months ago. There were no more strategy decks or award show scripts fobbed off on me. No more Friday night standoffs with my account team. Over time, my colleagues and I had come to an understanding of our roles. We had developed a rhythm and a rapport. They respected what I did as a writer and I, in turn, was a little less righteous and a little more flexible. We even had fun together now. There was also a new creative director and another writer, which helped lighten the workload and pressure. And with the growing team came—I wouldn't exactly call it "process"—but we figured out a way to get things done. It wasn't perfect, but it was easier than fighting. After all, what did we really need printed schedules, internal reviews, and project managers for? Things weren't *that* important. Things *would* get done. And at the end of the day, they miraculously did. Or maybe a little of that *laissez-faire* attitude was just rubbing off on me.

Meanwhile, all my friends kept asking, "What kind of discount do you get?" The glamour of working on such an esteemed brand must have some sweet perks, right? No one was more sorely disappointed than me to hear *rien*. With my newfound love for the brand, I really wanted a Louis Vuitton bag—the caramel-colored Antheia Hobo, made from sub-limely soft lambskin, to be exact. The monogram pattern was hand-quilted, and I knew it would be the most sophisticated ode to my time in Paris I could ever imagine. I *really* wanted that bag. But with no discount, and without an extra $3200 tucked in my panty drawer, I settled for the *Paris City Guide*, Vuitton's slender travel book, which was the only thing I could afford in the Champs-Élysées flagship.

But at least the job came with other perks. Things like pre-senting my work to Antoine Arnault, the luxury conglomer-ate president's lanky, blue-eyed son, at the hushed Pont Neuf headquarters that gave me a bird's-eye view of the Bateaux Mouches chugging up and down the Seine. Or sipping tea from heirloom china in the afternoon, and brandy from crystal tumblers in the evening, at the Vuitton family home in Asnières, a chichi suburb northwest of the city. Or peek-ing into Marc Jacobs's atelier from across the courtyard and sometimes seeing him at work there on his newest collection. I even got to breathe his creative genius one day when he got in the elevator with me at Pont Neuf, wearing his signature black kilt. *Oui, oui*, I was becoming quite comfortable work-ing for this legendary fashion house in Paris.

Every day was spent sitting at my desk—which had been in the Vuitton offices since winning the relaunch—researching the storied company's 155-year-old-history. I knew that Gaston, Louis's great-grandson, was a huge bibliophile with serious wanderlust and had laid the groundwork for the company's foray into publishing. I could now recognize the work of the power photography duo Mert Alas and Marcus Piggott as they had shot some of the company's sexiest ads. I could tell the difference between a Speedy, Keepall, and Neverfull, and knew the teal Vernis Alma was from the 2009 autumn collection, whereas the eclectic black Epi Alma came that following winter. Stephen Sprouse, Takashi Murakami, Ruben Toledo, Peter Marino—they were all names that never would have meant much to me otherwise, but I was now intimately familiar with as it was my job to know every last detail of the story of the House of Louis Vuitton.

Okay, so I didn't get a discount, and I shamelessly coveted that Antheia bag. But I was hooked. Someone had snuck me the Kool-Aid and I found myself nearly as excited to go to work as I was to discover that Pierre Hermé had a new macaron flavor to sink my teeth into.

— ✹ —

It had been eighteen months since that sunny summer when I took my Tour du Chocolat. On one evening during that visit, I had fortified myself from all the Vélib' riding and chocolate sampling with a flat *omelette des herbes* at Café Select in Montparnasse. I was so content sitting on the terrace, not so much with the food, which was pretty mediocre, but just with the moment. It was *l'heure bleu*, that magical twilight time when the light, suspended between day and night, is just otherworldly. I was laughing at the antics of Sally Jay Gorce, my new favorite American-in-Paris heroine from Elaine Dundy's fun and funny novel *The Dud Avocado*. I kept gazing across the busy boulevard to La Coupole, the famous brasserie where Josephine Baker had danced and Picasso, Hemingway, and Fitzgerald had dined, dreaming of the occasion to go. Now, a year and half later, I finally had it: I was invited to the Art Director's Club Awards Ceremony to receive a trophy for one of our Louis Vuitton websites.

Advertising is as self-congratulatory an industry as Hollywood. It's all about who works where, on what accounts, and what awards you've won. And it's thanks to these ceremonies that you can keep tabs on who's who. It's hardly the Oscars, but it's still a total schmoozefest.

I was looking forward to the night with anticipation, not so much for the pomp and fanfare but in nostalgic celebration of that summer evening I had spent across the street at Café Select. Back then, I'd had no idea that, one day, I'd not only be living in the City of Light, but I'd be enmeshed in a community there. It wasn't anything like the Lost Generation, but at least I belonged to *something*.

I idolized the Lost Generation, that wildly talented, free-spirited, financially struggling, and emotionally cantankerous group of writers, artists, and philosophizers from the 1920s and '30s who would stay up all night, smoking, drinking, and having intellectual spars. *A Moveable Feast, Girl before a Mirror, The Second Sex*—they had produced some of the most significant art and literature in my mind. They were the real deal. I knew Don Draper was giving ad folks a degree of coolness back home, but, as excited as I was for the evening, I was also a little sheepish to be going to the famed brasserie for an advertising trophy in the shadows of such artistic greatness. But fuck it, I was excited nonetheless.

Both Lionel, my macaron-loving partner with a super-sharp sense of design, and I were claiming victory, so we were allowed to bring dates. He naturally brought his wife, a large and lovely Mexican who, with perfectly lined eyelids and a flower in her hair, had successfully picked up that French *je ne sais quoi*. Jo, ever the good friend, was my date. The four of us met in front of the restaurant and entered the Art Deco splendor together.

The sprawling dining room, the size of about three tennis courts, buzzed with hundreds of people air-kissing and clinking champagne glasses. Waiters in black vests and bowties moved around briskly, setting pepper mills and bottles of Perrier on the tables, which were dressed in white linen. Cauldron-sized vases with knobby sticks of cherry blossoms decorated the backs of the brown velour banquettes. A fleet of green columns shot up to the ceiling, each adorned with a unique painting done by artists from the '20s, like Brancusi and Chagall. I breathed it all in. Such rich and artistic history.

And there we were—a French-Vietnamese with a mohawk, a five-foot-ten Mexican with flowers in her hair, an Aussie with a sly grin and funky eyeglasses, and me. We were a motley crew mingling with the *bon chic* mucky-mucks.

The scene cracked me up: men were decked out in tailored jackets and *baskets*; women wore billowy blouses and jeans—advertising hipsters with studiously disheveled hair, one and all. It could have been New York if not for all the scooter helmets that were toted around as proudly as the season's must-have fashion accessory from Colette. I cast my eye, trying to guess everyone's side talents and secret ambitions. The curse of being an advertising creative is you always dream of bigger things; every writer, art director, and producer has a half-written screenplay, shopped-around book proposal, music demo, or DJ gig. I looked at one woman with a chic Louise Brooks bob and matching strand of pearls, and imagined she crooned Ella and Edith at some subterranean jazz bar on the weekends. A guy nearby, stroking his salt and pepper stubble, rocking back and forth as he listened to his peers, I took for a budding director. Jo rescued me before serious self-loathing could kick in. "Should we mingle?"

"Sure. Except with whom?" I asked. "I don't know any of these people or understand a word of what they're saying."

"Eh, me either. Let's fake it. I think we've gotten good enough at it by now." She and I still commiserated about how being an expat in Paris was like living inside a bubble.

We could be seated at a dinner party, witnessing a confrontation on the Métro, shopping at a crowded street market—doing anything in the middle of this huge, international city—and remain utterly alone, trapped inside our heads. In your head, you could understand the voices; in the real world, words and conversations were just indecipherable background noise—beautiful, but meaningless all the same. But we made our way around the room in a valiant effort to look like we belonged. Like we *owned* that party. We watched the networking, flirting, and Gallic gesticulating—the things that translated quite easily into English—until we were asked to take our seats. The ceremony was about to begin.

The MC for the night was Ariel Wizman, a popular voice on French radio who was also one half of an electronic pop band. Accompanied by a waif in a cocktail dress (so original), he introduced a couple of creative directors who were brought up to the stage for brief speeches to tepid applause. Meanwhile, the dinner table was becoming laden with French goodies: bottles of champagne, then white, then red. Platters of mixed salad, then french fries, then sliced meat. The breadbaskets were regularly replenished, as were the bottles of still and sparkling water. My French skills had progressed, but not to the point of understanding phrases like, "And the trophy for best use of video in a corporate website goes to…," so I tuned out, eschewing the meat but enjoying the free-flowing champagne and *frites*. I wondered where Ezra Pound might have sat decades ago, supping on the brasserie's famed lamb curry. Or where Simone de Beauvoir and Sartre might have simmered, side by side, in their and others' curls of cigarette smoke. I was thinking that Hemingway or Picasso had maybe even been in the very seat where I was, just to the left of the bar, when Jo started nudging me.

"That's you, that's you!" Lionel was standing next to the table, waiting for me. Ariel had just announced our award. I shook myself from my sentimental reveries and, together, Lionel and I stormed the stage.

Through a blinding spotlight, I could see hundreds of bored eyes sizing us up while this skinny, coiffed Frenchman in his chocolate-brown bespoke suit, worn sans tie, oozed game show enthusiasm with the voice like molten chocolate. He was gushing into the microphone, doing his job for the night, which was to make us feel *très important*. He presented each of us with a trophy, shook our hands, and then directed us to exit, stage left. That was it—over in a flash and quite underwhelming. Until Melissa, my biggest fan in Paris, put it in perspective after seeing my blog posting and photo the next day: "Um, can we just take a moment…you are standing under spotlights, getting an award, on a circular stage, next to Ariel Wizman at La Coupole…way to make Paris your bitch, girl!"

——— ✳ ———

As much of a sweet freak as I am, by the time I finish a meal, I'm not so interested in dessert. I prefer my sweets midday or late night, consumed on an empty, eager stomach. But that night, the reward on top of the award was La Coupole's baba au rhum.

Baba au rhum is a popular French dessert that was on my radar, owing to my close proximity to Stohrer, the historic pâtisserie on rue Montorgueil where the dessert originated. Nicolas Stohrer, the young Polish pastry chef, had journeyed to Paris in 1725 along with the king of Poland's daughter, Marie Leszczynska, when she married King Louis XV. Five years after arriving in the court of Versailles, the royal chef opened this gorgeous pâtisserie. Two hundred and eighty years later, I was no stranger to its seductions.

Every time I stepped across the pâtisserie's name scrolled in gold across the turquoise tiled floor, I wanted to have a tea party. Naked maidens from the pastel frescoes by Paul Baudry, the same artist who painted the Garnier Opera's exquisite ceilings, stared down at me, and I couldn't help but channel Marie Antoinette and her three-foot-tall pompadours and five-foot-wide ball gowns. I'd float along the display case, rendered more and more helpless by all the pretty colors, elaborate constructions, and sheer embarrassment of options. There was the *charlotte aux framboises* with its perfectly plump berries, and tiramisu served exquisitely in a fine demi-chocolate shell. The *tartelette à l'orange* with a glossy sheen that made it look like an *art decoratif* rather than a little edible something, and the chocolate éclairs, with thick, shiny *glaçage*, had received *Le Figaro*'s nod for the city's best (a conclusion I concurred with). And then there was that funny golden, lumpish cake called the baba au rhum.

Nicolas Stohrer is said to have invented the dessert after splashing a dry Polish brioche with sweet Malaga wine to please the king. Stohrer's baba au rhum—still served in coffee-houses and restaurants around the world—has remained unchanged for centuries. And in addition to the original version, there are two other varieties: the Ali-Baba with raisins and the baba Chantilly, which is topped with fresh whipped cream.

— ✳ —

While I do ordinarily prefer my sweets as an afternoon *gouter* or a loyal companion in front of the TV at night, I loved the concept of dessert bars when they started popping up in New York. After all, they were the perfect excuse to just have dessert for dinner. I knew this was a totally valid philosophy after trying Pichet Ong's West Village dessert bar, p*ong.

Pichet has certainly enjoyed the sweet taste of success. After launching his pastry chef career at La Folie, a lovely French restaurant in San Francisco, and working at Todd English's acclaimed Olives in Boston, he took on Manhattan.

When he arrived in the city, he worked at successful restaurants like Jean Georges and Tabla. He started earning acco-
lades as the opening pastry chef of RM and consulting pastry
chef to Jean-Georges Vongerichten's popular restaurants, 66
and Spice Market. He told me that his own childhood was
the foundation for his novel approach to baking that relies
on flavors like yuzu, basil seed, and condensed milk—flavors
not seen on every dessert menu. "I grew up in Southeast Asia
and there's a lot of sweet and savory in Asian food. In general,
people don't think about it. But it's really nothing new for me
as a chef or an eater." With confidence in his unique skills,
he struck out on his own. In 2007, Pichet opened p*ong,
joining the nascent dessert bar trend. I went for my "Sweet
Freak" column, and it was love at first bite.

I chose a seat at the bar—the perfect cover for a solo diner.
But at p*ong, it had other advantages. Not only was I less
conspicuous (*Attention diners! Solo girl bingeing on cakes at
Table 8!*), but I could watch the creation and plating of the
gorgeous confections.

Out of the gate, I ordered the walnut-crusted Stilton
cheese soufflé, served with basil-arugula ice cream. Nuts,
cheese, and herbs. It was savory enough in my book to count
as a proper dinner item, and yet creamy and luscious enough
to trigger my sweet satisfaction.

The chèvre cheesecake croquette, up next, was light and
fluffy, another genre-bending dessert. Little cubes of diced

pineapple were the only giveaway that this wasn't what other people eat for supper.

And for the final course, I went whole-hog with the malted-chocolate Bavarian tart. It was a big hunk of creamy ganache, cloaked in chocolate crust and hiding beneath a layer of crunchy caramelized bananas. That chocolate-banana combination is one of my favorite things in the whole, wide world. With no reason for modesty, the rich tart was served alongside a delicate egg-shaped scoop of Ovaltine ice cream. I congratulated myself on choosing the perfect three-course dessert-dinner.

After that night, I was definitely smitten, not only with Pichet's refined desserts but also with his ambitious talent and unconventional approach to sweets. I became a one-woman groupie, following him over the years as he launched new businesses and consulted for others.

After p*ong, Pichet opened a bakery next door named Batch. I had faithfully waited months for it to debut and when it finally did, I went straight up to him and asked for his top five picks. This is always an interesting test for a baker or pastry chef. Do they plead that their desserts are like children and insist that they can't possibly have a favorite? Or do they act like true sweet freaks and rattle off their must-eats with a manic glint in their eye?

Pichet did neither. I could see the wheels turning in his head as his gaze darted around his gumdrop-sized bakery. I leaned in, licking my lips, eager for the chef's top picks. Then he began:

1. *The Valrhona chocolate chunk cookie*: I liked that Pichet was an ingredients snob. Fastidious bakers make better sweets.

2. *Chocolate dragon devil's food cupcake*: Again, made with Valrhona chocolate. That's chocolate on chocolate—a no-brainer in my book. The more chocolate, the better. Nope, you can never have too much chocolate.

3. *Ovaltine pudding*: With its silky, malty flavor and caramelized bananas, this unique dessert was too close to what I annihilated on my visit to p*ong. I knew its creamy deliciousness, but I wanted to try something new.

4. *Passion-fruit rice pudding*: I could appreciate that this was inspired directly from Pichet's childhood in Southeast Asia. But no matter how exotic dairy-free, coconut-vanilla rice pudding sweetened with tropical fruit sounded, I wasn't tempted.

5. *Carrot salted-caramel cupcake*: Ding! This last one got to me. Carrot cake is always served with cream cheese frosting. This was different. I liked the salted-caramel buttercream approach. I placed my order.

By this time, I had sampled dozens of cupcakes around the city, from banana at Billy's to pistachio at Sugar Sweet

Sunshine to Out of the Kitchen's classic yellow cake with chocolate frosting that tasted suspiciously, wonderfully, like Duncan Hines. They all had their merits. But none of them were the carrot salted-caramel cupcake from Batch.

The cake was so fresh, I could tell that it had only recently cooled from the oven. Shreds of carrot and hints of cinnamon gave the batter accents both spicy and savory, which were more complex than the plain chocolate or yellow cake of other cupcakes. The frosting also wowed me with discernible flavors: the delicately bitter taste of coffee extract and the tang of caramel. Then there was a lime cream-cheese filling hiding at the center: not exactly tart or sweet, but wholly unexpected and the most perfect complement to the cake and frosting. A dusting of Malden sea salt heightened all of the flavors. Happiness erupted from my tongue, and washed over every bit of me to the tips of my toes.

I was crushed when I heard Pichet closed both p*ong and Batch not long after my arrival in Paris. *Crushed.* But never one to remain idle, Pichet had moved on to the next sweet spot called, well, Spot. On one of my trips home to New York, I dutifully revisited him. It was more of a hybrid bakery-bar than two separate businesses as p*ong and Batch had been. Otherwise, though, his sweet-savory creations were on delicious display. I sampled soft cheesecake, served elegantly spilling out of a highball glass turned on its side, with bits of huckleberry compote, crushed walnuts, and lemon foam. The white miso semifreddo, two fine slices of olive oil cake, which sat on a bed of crushed almonds alongside raspberry sorbet. And lastly, the über-rich chocolate ganache cake, which was similar to the dish I'd had years earlier at p*ong, but was now paired with green tea ice cream, crackly caramel crunches, and malted chocolate bits. Spot lived up to its predecessors. It was a different establishment, but it still had Pichet's magic.

———— ✳ ————

The more things changed in New York, I realized, the more they stayed the same in Paris. While Pichet represented everything edgy and innovative in New York's dessert circles, history reigned in Paris.

Back at La Coupole, I bit into the glistening baba au rhum, the brioche oozing and squishy, a little bit obscene. The rum-soaked cake before me had royal origins and had remained unchanged for centuries. It was the perfect celebratory dessert for that night; a delicious *fin de soirée*. With the potent punch of alcohol rolling across my tongue, I absorbed the ghosts of Paris's past, and took a last look at the scene before me. I may have been a bit sheepish that my big night at La Coupole had been about an advertising website, not some revolutionary belief or profound novel that would stand the test of time. But it was still something, and I was still in love with my job.

MORE
Sweet Spots
ON THE
MAP

Only in New York can you find small restaurants devoted to sweets. When the dessert bar trend took off, I was excited. The rest of the city, apparently not so much. Most shuttered within a year of opening. But two notably remain: Chika Tillman's original dessert bar, ChikaLicious, in the East Village, is still going strong and has spawned a takeaway bakery across the street. (More great cupcakes! And brioche bread pudding! Miam!) And the Japanese dessert bar, Kyotofu, in Hell's Kitchen, goes heavy and delicious on the soy.

I'm admittedly more of a sweets snacker than a dessert person, but the final course in Parisian restaurants is always a thrill. I first tried baba au rhum at Bistrot Paul Bert in the 11e, where they actually plunk a bottle of rum on the table so you can douse your dessert with more spirits (I was with Michael, and we, of course, doused our cake beaucoup). The caramel soufflé at l'Atelier de Joël Robuchon at the head of the Champs-Élysées is light, lovely, and utterly transporting. And at Chez Janou in the Marais and Chez l'Ami Jean in the 7e, giant mixing bowls of chocolate mousse and rice pudding are brought to the table, tempting you to take just a little more…just a little more…okay, just a little more…

—[CHAPTER 12]—

FRENCH TOAST OR PAIN PERDU, THAT IS THE QUESTION

I had become like a broken record, playing the same questions over and over in my mind. Fate or control? New York or Paris? Breakfast or dessert?

Let me explain. For over a year, I had been straddling two worlds: Paris and New York. I now saw life in stark dualities, everything an either-or option. Did I want to be an expat or a local? American or French? Did I want to run with my advertising career, now so fulfilling, or funnel more energy to magazine writing, as I had thought I would do while living abroad? I also debated whether I should live more like a proper Parisian and create sacred weekends devoted to relaxation and pleasure, or keep at it like a good New Yorker and knock things off my to-do list. Why *was* I in Paris? What was the real reason I was there? Or was there no reason at all—maybe it was just dumb, wonderful luck. *Was Paris my fate?* Since I couldn't crack the question, I thought it was something a couple girlfriends and a pitcher of beer could help me with.

—— ✳ ——

They say you have to live in a new city at least a year before you feel like you belong. Sure enough, that spring, I could consider myself more of an in-the-know local than a lonely outsider. When someone stopped me in the street to ask for directions (*Vraiment? I look like a Parisienne?*), I not only understood what they were saying, but I also knew my way around well enough to know where they needed to go. And I could tell them *en français*. (If I was completely nonsensical in my response, they were always kind enough to thank me before getting on their way.) My cheesemonger (yes, I had a "cheesemonger" and I loved saying that) recognized me to the point that he'd migrate toward the brebis, a beautifully mild and creamy sheep's milk cheese from the Basque region, knowing I'd only occasionally stray from my usual order to opt for *une tranche de Comté* instead. The pâtisserie spreadsheet I had arrived in Paris with had not only grown prodigiously, but had also been tackled impressively. And the real sign that I was now a local? I had an expanding circle of friends whom I adored.

Jo and I had grown closer over the months working at Ogilvy. Although we worked on separate accounts, in different buildings, we still managed lunch weekly and would bond over shared office politics and gossip. Along the way, I had met Sarah at a little soirée of Rachel's, whom I had met while whipping the eggs, butter, sugar, and cream together for a plum clafoutis at a cooking class. Sarah was a young up-and-coming writer from New York. Rachel hailed from London and was a self-described "food creative" who wrote cookbooks and threw themed dinner parties—Jackie O! Communist Germany! The '80s!—when she wasn't working at Bob's Juice Bar, a small *cantine* opened by a fellow New Yorker near Canal Saint-Martin that served bagels and smoothies. Needless to say, I was delighted to connect with kindred spirits who loved food, fashion, art, and *la belle vie en Paris* as much as I did. There were scads of us expats in the city, and in hindsight, it was inevitable that we'd fall into the small and overlapping communities that we did.

Still, when I'd first moved to Paris, I wanted nothing more than to be on the French-local side of my self-inflicted divide. I didn't want to become part of an expat gang who ate cheeseburgers and watched football games at Irish pubs at odd hours of the night. Instead, I envisioned hours spent around the kitchen table of someone's garret apartment, where there would be abundant wine and cheese and baguettes splayed on the table. I'd regale my new French friends with my expat antics, told in an oh-so-charming American accent. The men would wink at me, and the women would want to spend

Saturdays shopping with me at Le Bon Marché. I could even see myself joining them in the occasional cigarette.

Needless to say, my little Franco-fantasies never transpired. And after a year of clicking with nary a Frenchie the same way I did the Anglophones, I was firmly in the expat camp. On one hand, it felt like failure, that I had moved to a foreign city and never managed to assimilate. If only I had worked harder at my vocabulary exercises or learned to flirt like a Frenchwoman. But practically, I was grateful and relieved to be part of a group. That I could speak my mind and be understood, literally and emotionally. And that I had girlfriends to go out with on a Saturday night!

—— ✳ ——

We were actually on our second pitcher of beer when I opened up the fate debate to Jo and Sarah. We were at The Bottle Shop, a rowdy bar in the eleventh arrondissement that was filled with…Anglophones. We loved it because everyone stood around the bar, instead of cloistering themselves at individual café tables. It was actually possible to meet people at a bar like The Bottle Shop. Besides, most Parisian bartenders wore pastel-colored v-necks and had waists smaller than mine. Here, they were buff, tattooed *dudes*.

"Do you believe in fate?" I asked innocently, eyeing the bartender's bicep. Even though tatts aren't my thing, I can appreciate a nice, strong arm.

Jo looked thoughtfully through her oversized Ray-Ban frames. She and Cedric had sped so quickly through the traditional relationship stages that it was totally normal for her to spend Saturday nights with the girls again instead of at home, in cozy coupledom. "Well, I used to believe in fate," she started carefully. "Until I realized that if you believe in fate, then you're sort of relinquishing control over your own life." She started speaking faster, really rolling with it. "If everything happens for a reason, then it's like you really have nothing to do with where you are in your life—as if all your choices, actions, and decisions have nothing to do with your success." As a Class A control freak, I had to cede the point to her (Fate, 0; Control, 1). "And," she added for final emphasis, "I'd like to think that I am where I am because of *me*."

"Yeah, I think fate is sorta bullshit." At just twenty-five years old, Sarah had a razor-sharp tongue. If ever you wanted a healthy debate or a contrarian opinion, she was your girl. "I mean, what about really crappy things that happen to people? Like a guy who gets hit by a bus and leaves a family behind? Or you lose your job and health insurance when the economy goes south? You're telling me that's fate? That's supposed to happen? Or kids born in the Congo to see their parents slaughtered—*really?* That's *supposed* to happen according to some divine orchestration?" (*Touché!* Fate, 0; Control, 2.)

"I know, I know. It makes no sense and can be maddening, but isn't that also the point? That we *don't* know, and that we don't have control? But that things just happen because they're supposed to? You don't always have the reasons or answers."

"Meh…" I noticed Sarah's eyes also straying to the bartender's bicep. "It's bullshit."

"Yeah, how do you account for the fact that I was born and raised in Australia, and today, here I am, living in Paris? It's not some higher power. It's because I *wanted* to leave. It was totally my doing, man." Jo licked her lips and pushed her glasses back up on her nose. "And like Sarah said, how do you justify all the tragedies and death, then? I just can't believe those things are meant to be."

They were both getting riled up now, and I knew on some level they were right. (Fate, 0; Control, 3.) There are devastating tragedies, inexplicable events, and freaks of nature that simply can't be rationalized. But I couldn't shake the feeling that Paris was my fate, and I was hungry for validation. I pressed on. "But aside from life's tragedies, what about those instant connections we feel with certain people and places? And what about the idea of being in the right place at the right time? Maybe it is all part of some greater cosmic plan that we're not necessarily aware of, but we should just trust." Those things had always bugged me—the way it seemed you knew someone even though you had only just met them. Or you felt a deep connection to a place you'd never even been before, like you'd been there in a dream or something. It had to be fate, right? (*Oui!* Fate, 1; Control, 3.)

As Jo and Sarah now delved deeper into the debate, I was flashing back on my relationship with the City of Light and Dark Chocolate, now in its seventeenth year. I fell in love with Paris (and the Nutella street crepes...*mon dieu!*) during my college semester abroad. But as smitten as I was, I was young and dutifully returned home at the end of my semester. A few years later, when I lived with Max in San Francisco, I wanted to cash in my 401(k) so he and I could move over together and be romantic bohemians who spent our days writing and making out in public gardens. But he just laughed good-naturedly at the idea. So I carried on year after year with life in the States, forever obsessed with that magical city on the other side of the ocean. I read books by Janet Flanner and Gertrude Stein, watched Eric Rohmer and Jean Renoir movies, and I spent countless hours listening to Michel Thomas on cassette.

Then the tipping point came in 2008, with my Tour du Chocolat. Living like a local for a week, Vélib'ing all over town, visiting chocolatiers—*that* was the life! When I returned to New York after that, I was chatting with an old colleague who was taking a leave of absence to live in the Marais for three months—a bold and exciting idea that had never even crossed my mind. But one morning not long after, I had a revelation at Balthazar, my favorite restaurant in Soho that's, unsurprisingly, the perfect replication of a French bistro, right down to the billowy, buttery croissants.

I was breakfasting with one of my old creative directors and midconversation—*midsentence*—something suddenly, inexplicably turned over in my head. I thought that *oui*, I too should take a leave of absence to spend time in Paris. I decided I was going to do it the following spring. And then, just a few weeks later, Allyson walked through my office door (Fate, 2; Control, 3).

But if Paris was my fate, what was I supposed to be getting out of it? I had come over with romantic visions of meeting a tarte tatin prince and getting a big, fat book contract to write about sweets. I was going to be Paris's pastry doyenne. But a year later, I was still single and had no publishing deal (that, happily, was to come later). The fantasy life had long been tempered by reality, and I knew that living in a magical city came with a price. I was looking for some sort of grand epiphany that would explain everything. Like what if I had gone to Madrid instead of Paris for my semester abroad? What if I had never taken my Tour du Chocolat? What if I hadn't been in my office that day Allyson came looking, and she asked someone else about the job? And…what if something monumental was in fact waiting for me—I just needed to stay in Paris another few months to discover it? What if…?

A year ago, I'd felt I had nothing to do with my Parisian stint happening—Allyson had walked into my office, not the other way around. But maybe it *had* been me. Maybe it was something like *guided fate*. Maybe it was possible to want something so much, for so long, without even consciously realizing it, that finally fate had to listen and cooperate. Maybe I was in control of my own fate, steering myself, if only subconsciously, toward the life I was meant to live? Maybe Jo and Sarah *and* I were all right. (Fate, 2.5; Control, 2.5?)

With that thought, I decided to drop the agonizing debate and just enjoy the moment of being at a rowdy bar on a Saturday night. *You're a better dreamer than philosopher*, I told myself. *Let the answers remain mysterious.* The DJ was spinning Motown. The smell of beer was both cloying and delicious. There were cute boys in the room. Things were beginning to get good.

"How about that bartender's body?" I asked, to the appreciative nods and sighs of my friends.

— ✳ —

But of course my mind wouldn't rest so easily. I had a decision to make. I was an American in Paris—an American *in love* with Paris—and yet I still couldn't decide where my heart, my *life*, belonged. I was torn between loving Paris and missing New York. It seemed the grass was always greener and the sweets sweeter on the other side of the Atlantic.

Partly what had gotten me through the months since my last visit home was the knowledge that my time in Paris was limited. My second CDD—*contrat à durée déterminée*—expired at the end of June, just a few months down the road, and I had been planning on returning home then. I drew comfort from this (*au revoir, lonely nights!*) and was even more motivated to make the most of every day in Paris, knowing it wasn't forever.

But suddenly, I wasn't so sure. Was I really done with Paris? (*One's never done with Paris*...a little voice inside my head chastised.) Would my life be better back in New York? (*Debatable, in and of itself...*) Did I have to make a choice? (*Yes, otherwise drive yourself utterly insane.*) If coming to Paris had been fate, guided or otherwise, I realized at least I was in total control of what happened next. I could choose to sign another short-term contract, or maybe even go full-time in Paris and remain indefinitely. My choice.

My heart had been telling me one thing for months: to return to my family and friends back home. But summer, my favorite season, was on the horizon. Did I really want to leave and miss the 10:00 p.m. sunsets that provided several extra hours for Vélib' riding and drinking rosé along the canal? To deny myself a few more months of morning pastries, wonderfully billowy and blissfully warm from the oven? And what about work? Writing for Louis Vuitton, in Paris, was about as good as it was going to get. Did I really want to walk away? No. And yes. Yes and no. I simply couldn't decide. So I started creating checklists, debating which of these two decadent cities was the right choice:

PLEASURE OR SUCCESS?

Long, leisurely dinners. Dozing in the sun along the Seine. Sitting with friends and watching the world go by. In Paris, you dream, you pontificate, you light another cigarette. You're supposed to just *be*.

In New York, you can't just be. But you can be anything or anyone you want.

BEAUTY OR ENERGY?

Of course I had always known how dazzling Paris is. But to actually live there and walk the streets—with the massive plane trees and ancient cobblestones, the rose-tinted street lamps, the green bookstalls, and golden limestone façades— well, the French know a little something about seduction.

But in New York, you're swept away by everything and everyone around you: pedestrians, taxis, buses, street ven- dors, blinking neon signs, little dogs, big dogs, and, oh, the freaks everywhere! To walk the streets of New York is to know what it means to feel *alive*.

PLAT DU JOUR OR TREND OF THE MOMENT?

Thick, white spears of asparagus. Plump, juicy duck breasts. Eggs with neon orange yolks. *The salted butter.* With some of the purest ingredients and most celebrated recipes and cook- ing techniques in the world, there's little better than dining in Paris. You linger forever, indulge in course after course, bite after bite, while keeping pace with lovely regional wines and being charmed by the wait staff (if they're not bristling at having to work).

But in New York, you get a scene served alongside dinner. You get madcap creations and unique techniques, ever-surprising menus and colorful creations. The only problem is, you're also guilted into ordering more alcohol, more food, more, more, more to jack up the bill. ("That's it? You know, the plates are pretty small here…") Then you're pressured to eat quickly so they can cram in as much business as possible that night. And don't forget to tip your actor/artist/model/carpenter/hipster waiter 20 percent. Or else.

Chinon or Sidecar?

Ah, French wine. I had developed the habit of drinking a glass—Chinon, Bordeaux, Côtes du Rhône, *peu import*—nearly every night. And whenever I traveled home to New York, I was reminded of how lucky I was to do so. In Manhattan, the average glass of wine starts at an outrageous $12 compared to €3 or €4 in Paris. And that's for a glass of mediocrity.

But, oh, how I missed a good cocktail. I was lucky to live near Experimental in Paris, where the drinks were as delicious as they were creative. But if I had a centime for every lousy sidecar I had, I'd be a very rich girl indeed.

MACARON OR CUPCAKE?

Needless to say, I had sampled some of the best sweets in both New York and Paris. At one time, I thought there was nothing better than Momofuku's cornflake, marshmallow, chocolate chip cookie. Until I bit into Pierre Hermé's exquisite chocolate and salted caramel *Plenitude Individuel.* I thought I'd miss the blueberry-studded muffins from Thé Adoré. But then I fell for Du Pain et Des Idées's flaky croissants and escargots. From cupcakes to cocoa, my head spun from the comparisons, and my internal debate raged on:

Bagels or baguettes?

Peanut butter or Speculoos?

Taxis or Vélib's?

Manolos or Repettos?

Oversized sunglasses or oversized scarves?

Diners or cafés?

Downtown or Left Bank?

Empire State or Eiffel Tower?

Bergdorf or Colette?

Carrie Bradshaw or Charlotte Gainsbourg?

New York or Paris?

Should I stay, or should I go?

From every angle it was a draw—and I was exhausted. The mental acrobatics, zinging back and forth, yes or no, stay or go, were getting me nowhere. Maybe I'd just have to let fate decide, after all.

— ✴ —

As for the last question on my mind, it wasn't exactly keeping me up at night, but it taunted me every time I went for Sunday brunch.

No, not the classic eggs-or-pancakes dilemma (salty or sweet?). But just where in the hell was all the French toast? *Bien sûr*, French toast was the king of brunch in New York. But on every menu in Paris, it was conspicuously absent. Were they hiding it? Boycotting it? Oblivious to this delicious dish that bandied their own nationality in its name (even though France had nothing to do with its origins)? Come to find out, in Paris, the equivalent of French toast is *le pain perdu*. It's served as dessert, not breakfast. And it's divine.

— ✴ —

With *le pain perdu*, you already start with the best bread in the world: a simple French baguette. And then it just gets better from there.

Similar to baba au rhum, *le pain perdu* was the result of salvaging dry cake—or in this case, a stale baguette. It's said to have been invented by Romans who couldn't afford to waste a crumb of food. By moistening and heating old bread, they could revive and savor it for another meal. Granted, stale bread soaked in a mix of dairy is a little less sexy than the baba's sweet wine and brioche folklore. But what *le pain perdu* lacks in romanticism it more than makes up for in decadence.

You slice and soak the baguette pieces in a custard batter of milk or cream, eggs, sugar, and, depending on the recipe, perhaps fresh vanilla, cinnamon, or other spices for up to thirty minutes. This soaking gives the bread an extra dense and heavy texture—like bread pudding or almond croissants, two of my favorite carb-filled indulgences. Then it's cooked on a hot, buttered *poêle*, or frying pan, until it's golden, crusty, and caramelized. Finally, it's topped with all manner of naughtiness, from caramel ice cream to berry sauce to *crème Chantilly*—or all of the above, as was the case with my decadent dessert at the cozy two-story Saint-Germain restaurant, Au 35.

In the States, there's a little less fanfare around French toast. The bread isn't soaked so much as quickly dipped, and then it's normally topped with just butter and maple syrup. Unless you know where to go.

— ❋ —

Before Paris, I had fallen for a seriously ridiculous version of French toast in New York. Ben and I loved eating shamelessly together, had been momentarily delusional, and thought we'd get into one of the most popular Sunday-brunch destinations in the city—Gabrielle Hamilton's restaurant, Prune—at exactly high noon. But after we were told the wait was ninety minutes, not even the promise of the 33 LP-sized Dutch pancake or eggs Benedict on a delicate English muffin could sway us. We regained our wits and decided to seek a new option. Not even half a block down the gritty East Village street, we stumbled upon a new spot: Joe Doe.

Started by a young couple from Long Island, Joe Dobias and Jill Schulster, the restaurant is tiny (with room for just twenty-six), rustic, and filled with intimate charms. Antique furniture and framed family photos decorate the walls and bar, while an open kitchen in the back corner makes it feel like you're in Joe and Jill's own home.

I don't know if it was all so quaint and pastoral that I thought I could actually smell country air as we situated our-selves at the table in the front window or what, but I ordered granola. More likely, I had been bingeing on sweets all week and was now just trying to be "good." Whatever the reason, it was silly. Not even two minutes later, the table next to us got their meals, and that's when I saw it: a platter with two honking slabs of caramelized bread, drowning in a sea of syrup, buried under a pile of bananas and whipped cream, and dusted with a delicate layer of confectionary sugar. It was Joe's challah bread French toast topped with bananas Foster.

"Um? Excuse me?" I flagged down our waitress. "Is it too late to change my order?"

She followed my gaze, which was desperately resting on my neighbor's French toast, and took pity on me. "I don't think so. Let me just check." She walked back to the open kitchen and consulted with Joe. His eyes remained planted on the stove, his hands busy with tongs and spatulas. I realized I was holding my breath until the waitress turned around and gave me the thumbs up from across the room. I exhaled. *Yes!* I was spared that miserable feeling of restaurant order remorse.

Chef Joe evidently understands the power he wields in the kitchen. "There has never been a better topping," the very opinionated chef said of his New Orleans-inspired Foster sauce, made with brown sugar, butter, and dark Meyer's rum. I had to agree with his declaration. Twenty minutes later, when Ben and I were digging into our dishes, I was pretty sure I'd never had French toast quite so soddenly delicious.

It wasn't just the bananas Foster topping. It was the whole package. "The bread is super important," Joe instructed. "Originally I was a brioche guy, but a few years back, I discovered challah bread." He cuts thick square slices from a giant loaf and does a quick ten to fifteen second soak in a batter of eggs, cream, milk, cinnamon, and vanilla extract. Unlike the stale baguettes used in France that better absorb moisture, the fluffy challah will get soggy if it soaks too long.

Then it all comes together: a custard-soaked plate of carbs beneath a wonderfully sweet sauce, sliced and caramelized bananas, plus whipped cream for good measure. "It should be colossal in order to fit the brunch bill!" Indeed, it was. It was a meal in and of itself. There was no way anything that big and decadent could have been stomached as dessert after a proper dinner in Paris.

— ✹ —

The curse of being an expat, I realized, is that you belong to two cities and, as a result, neither entirely. I had been asking myself either-or questions, but the answers were not black and white but a million shades of Parisian gray. I could have French toast for breakfast and *pain perdu* for dessert. Live in Paris and love New York. Or vice versa. While straddling two cities had made me see life in stark dualities, it had also given me the chance to indulge in the best of both worlds. Maybe I *could* have my gâteau and eat it too.

MORE
Sweet Spots
ON THE
MAP

I think I missed French toast so much in Paris because the options in New York are so ridiculous and delicious. At Extra Virgin in the West Village, the caramelized bread is topped with bananas (also caramelized) and mascarpone (God, I love mascarpone). And at Good, also in the West Village, they stuff their French toast with banana cream cheese. Miam.

The trendy Hotel Amour in the 9e does serve le pain perdu *for Sunday brunch, but the way to go in Paris is to order it for dessert. L'Epicuriste, in the residential 15e, tops their* le pain perdu *with a nice pear compote, while at J'Go in Saint-Germain, there is no topping, but the custardy, crusty, caramelized bread is heaven on a plate.*

CHAPTER 13

ONE OF LIFE'S BEST SURPRISES: THE BAKER'S DOZEN

I was late to meet Melissa. We'd now known each other a year, but it was more like eighteen in "expat years" and I knew she was a friend for life. We were going to see *Sex and the City 2* on the Champs-Élysées and, as excited as I was to see Carrie, Miranda, Charlotte, and Samantha whooping it up in Abu Dhabi, I couldn't quite muster the enthusiasm. My contract deadline was fast approaching, and I still didn't know what to do. Was Paris really my dream life and the most important place to be? Or did I belong in New York?

On the Paris side, I had my jump-started career, the city's beauty and architecture, budding new friendships, more European travels, and macarons. In New York, I had my friends and family, my East Village apartment (still furnished, waiting for me), a comfortable lifestyle, a culture in which I felt a sense of belonging, and cupcakes. After all the months of internally debating what to do, I was no closer to an answer.

But as I Vélib'ed across the magnificent Place de la Concorde, now one of my favorite and most symbolic places in the city, the clouds parted, sending dazzling rays of sunshine in a 180-degree arc. I had a cache of bonbons in my bag just as I had nearly two years earlier when I pedaled this same path on my Tour du Chocolat. The sky behind the clouds was the most brilliant blue. I knew at that moment that I was truly seeing the light—that staying in Paris, if only for another six months, was the right thing to do.

I thought of the pure happiness that coursed through my veins whenever I rode one of those Vélib's. The automatic smile that lit my face when I turned the corner and saw the Place Vendome in the morning. The ecstasy of that very last, hot and melty bite of a Nutella street crepe.

I thought of the hours I'd spent around different dinner tables and the number of *boulangeries* and pâtisseries that had seduced me with their warm baking smells and visions of bright, beautiful cakes. I thought of the infinite strolls I had taken through Paris and the distances I had traveled beyond the city's borders. I thought about sipping cocoa with Mom and Bob at Angelina, of touring the kitchen of Du Pain et Des Idées with Isa, and of introducing Chris, Dad, the girls, and all my other friends who had visited me to the unforgettable flavors and exquisite pleasures of Paris. There were the French lessons and cooking classes. The professional challenges and dating follies. And, as unbearable as all those lonely, soul-searching nights had been, they were now deeply embedded parts of me—war wounds. Coming to Paris had changed my life. Maybe in a way that I couldn't entirely articulate or define, but in a very important way nevertheless.

I parked the Vélib' and ran to meet Melissa in the line stretching up the Champs. Wow, who knew chic Parisiennes were so devoted to the antics of fabulous New Yorkers? I saw Mel and waved. I was smiling. I had a spring in my step again. I had finally made my decision and sealed my fate. I was going to stay in Paris…if only for just a little while longer.

The sweets shared in this book are by no means all Paris and New York have to offer. Nor are they necessarily my all-time favorites. (I mean, c'mon—I've barely even mentioned chocolate éclairs or fudgy brownies or ice cream sundaes or tarte tatin or...) But they each played a memorable part in my story. If I had to offer my top-ten sweets for each city, well, the lists would look something like this:

Paris

1. A good, ol' oozing Nutella street crepe.
2. La Folie at La Pâtisserie des Rêves: the heft and texture of this squat pastry are pure magic. The doughy, whipped brioche is piped full of vanilla pastry cream that has a hint of rum raisin. Topped with praline crumble and a touch of confectioner's sugar, it's unbelievably yummy.
3. The insanely addictive praluline from Pralus Chocolatier in the Marais. This buttery, chewy, crunchy, caramelized sweet brioche, chock-full of almonds from Valencia and crushed hazelnuts from Piedmont, is meant for at least four people. But I would eat an entire one myself.
4. The sweet little strawberry Coeur from Coquelicot

in Montmartre. Relatively modest in size—just four or five bites—but this petite cake has a pitch-perfect texture that's both spongy and moist.

5. A chocolate éclair from Stohrer. The crisp pastry shell envelopes an über generous chocolaty custard filling and is slathered with a sweet chocolate *glaçage*. It's a serious sugar rush.

6. Angelina's stick-to-your-teeth *chocolat chaud*. It's like sipping melted truffles. In a tearoom that Coco Chanel used to frequent.

7. Speaking of truffles, Jean-Paul Hévin's truffles are *le mieux*. And his *mendiants*. And his cakes. Hévin = heaven in my book.

8. The rice pudding at Chez l'Ami Jean. I never would have thought I'd care a lick about rice pudding. But a dinner at Café Constant made me reconsider, and a later dinner at Chez l'Ami Jean changed everything. Served in a massive bowl with sides of candied granola and salted caramel cream, this is an unforgettable dessert.

9. The Plenitude Individuel from Pierre Hermé. While his macarons are, *oui*, divine, this little cake is transporting. Fluffy chocolate mousse under a dark chocolate shell. Kissed by salted caramel. Adorned with tiles of more chocolate. It's gorgeous, exquisite, and delicious.

10. An almond croissant from Boulangerie Julien. When my friend Ben and I split one of these, we were giggling like school kids in the middle of rue Saint-Honoré. Fresh and flaky, slightly chewy and caramelized at the edges, heavy with almond paste and lightly dusted with powdered sugar and slivered almond. I mean, how can something be allowed to taste so good?

New York

1. The six ounces of chocolaty, oaty goodness that is Levain's chocolate chip walnut cookie. It's true, it's tough to declare a favorite in this category, but if I had to eat one chocolate chip cookie for the rest of my life, I'd go with Levain's.

2. A *pain au chocolat* from Pâtisserie Claude. Early morning. When they're still warm and melty.

3. Any one of Pichet Ong's cupcakes. Sadly, the carrot salted-caramel cupcake has vanished along with his bakery, Batch (though, shhhh, I have the recipe to make at home when serious cravings kick in). But there are plenty of other dreamy options at Spot, including berry chocolate, mocha caramel with Malden sea salt, vanilla yuzu lemon, and vanilla caramel Viennese coffee.

4. The chocolate bread pudding from the mobile

Dessert Truck. It's warm, spongy decadence with a molten middle, and topped with crème anglaise. What more could you ask for?

5. Although I say I'm more of a sweets snacker than a dessert girl, I will happily put away multiple desserts, after dinner, at Gramercy Tavern. While the menu changes seasonally, a couple past standouts include butterscotch bread pudding with pear sorbet and chocolate pudding with toasted brioche croutons and caramel.

6. Teuscher champagne truffles. This feels a bit like cheating as Teuscher is a Swiss chocolatier, not homegrown in Manhattan. But these decadent truffles make my heart go pitter-patter.

7. Crack pie at Momofuku. Because crack always keeps you coming back.

8. City Bakery's peanut butter cookies. As opposed to the giant chocolate chip varietals, these are wee little scoops of peanut butter batter, baked to moist, savory perfection. *Merci*, Maury!

9. The chocolate blackout cake doughnut from Doughnut Plant. Chocolate. Blackout. Enough said.

10. A slice of banana cake with cream cheese frosting from Billy's. Cupcakes are AJ's favorite, but sometimes you just want to sit down with a slab of dense, moist cake, slathered in frosting. At least I do.

LIST OF BAKERIES

* ⋯⋯⋯⋯⋯⋯⋯⋯⋯⋯⋯⋯⋯⋯⋯⋯⋯⋯⋯ *

PARIS

A l'Étoile d'Or
30, rue Fontaine (9e)
01 48 74 59 55

A la Flûte Gana
226, rue des Pyrenées (20e)
01 43 58 42 62
www.gana.fr

A la Mère de Famille
33-35, rue du Faubourg
    Montmartre (9e)
01 47 70 83 69

82, rue Montorgueil (2e)
01 53 40 82 78

39, rue du Cherche Midi (6e)
01 42 22 49 99

47, rue Cler (7e)
01 45 55 29 74

59, rue de la Pompe (16e)
01 45 04 73 19

107, rue Jouffroy d'Abbans (17e)
01 47 63 52 94
www.lameredefamille.com

Angelina
226, rue de Rivoli (1er)
01 42 60 82 00
www.groupe-bertrand.com/
    angelina.php

Au 35
35, rue Jacob (6e)
01 42 60 23 04

Blé Sucre
7, rue Antoine Vollon (12e)
01 43 40 77 73

Bob's Juice Bar
15, rue Lucien Sampaix (10e)
09 50 06 36 18
www.bobsjuicebar.com

The Bottle Shop
5, rue Trousseau
01 43 14 28 04
www.myspace.com/thebottleshop

Café Constant
139, rue Saint-Dominique (7e)
01 47 53 73 34
www.cafeconstant.com

Chez Janou
2, rue Roger Verlomme (3e)
01 42 72 28 41
www.chezjanou.com

Chez Jeannette
47, rue du Faubourg-Saint-Denis
01 47 70 30 89
www.chezjeannette.com

Chez l'Ami Jean
27, rue Malar (7e)
01 47 05 86 89
www.amijean.eu

Columbus Café
25, rue Vieille du Temple (4e)
01 42 72 20 11
www.columbuscafe.com

Coquelicot
24, rue des Abbesses (18e)
01 46 06 18 77
www.coquelicot-montmartre.com

Cosi
54, rue de Seine (6e)
01 46 33 35 36
www.getcosi.com

Cupcakes & Co.
25, rue de la Forgé Royale (11e)
01 43 67 16 19
www.cupcakesandco.fr

Cupcakes Berko
23, rue Rambuteau (4e)
01 40 29 02 44

31, rue Lepic (18e)
01 42 62 94 12
www.cupcakesberko.com

Du Pain et Des Idées

34, rue Yves Toudic (10e)
01 42 40 44 52
www.dupainetdesidees.com

Eggs & Co.

11, rue Bernard Palissy (6e)
01 45 44 02 52
www.eggsandco.fr

Eric Kayser

33, rue Danielle Casanova (1er)
01 42 97 59 29

16, rue des Petits Carreaux (2e)
01 42 33 76 48

8, rue Monge (5e)
01 44 07 01 42

14, rue Monge (5e)
01 44 07 17 81

1, boulevard du Montparnasse (6e)
01 47 83 75 39

10, rue de l'Ancienne
   Comedie (6e)
01 43 25 71 60

87, rue d'Assas (6e)
01 43 54 92 31

18, rue du Bac (7e)
01 42 61 27 63

85, boulevard Malesherbes (8e)
01 45 22 70 30

Lafayette Gourmet (9e)

309, rue du Faubourg
   Saint-Antoine (11e)
01 43 79 01 76

77, Quai Panhard et Levassor (13e)
01 56 61 11 06

87, rue Didot (14e)
01 45 42 59 19

79, rue du Commerce (15e)
01 44 19 88 54

79, avenue Mozart (16e)
01 42 88 03 29

19, avenue des Ternes (17e)
01 43 80 23 28
www.maison-kayser.com

Experimental Cocktail Club

37, rue Saint-Saveur (2e)
01 45 08 88 09
www.experimental
   cocktailclub.com

Fauchon
24-30, place de la Madeleine (8e)
01 70 39 38 00
www.fauchon.com

Gaya Rive Gauche
44, rue du Bac (7e)
01 45 44 73 73
www.pierre-gagnaire.com

Gérard Mulot
6, rue du Pas de la Mule (3e)
01 45 26 85 77

76, rue de Seine (6e)
01 42 78 52 17

93, rue de la Glacière (13e)
01 45 81 39 09
www.gerard-mulot.com

H.A.N.D.
(Have A Nice Day)
39, rue Richelieu (1er)
01 40 15 03 27

Hotel Amour
8, rue de Navarin (9e)
01 48 78 31 80
www.hotelamourparis.fr

Hugo et Victor
7, rue Gomboust (1er)
01 42 96 10 20

40, boulevard Raspail (7e)
01 44 39 97 73
www.hugovictor.com

Il Gelato
65, boulevard Saint-Germain (5e)
01 46 34 26 53

J'Go
4, rue Drouot (9e)
01 40 22 09 09

6, rue Clément (6e)
01 43 26 19 02
www.lejgo.com

Jacques Genin
133, rue de Turenne (3e)
01 45 77 29 01

Jean-Paul Hévin
231, rue Saint-Honoré (1er)
01 55 35 35 96

3, rue Vavin (6e)
01 43 54 09 85

23 bis, avenue de la
    Motte-Picquet (7e)

01 45 51 77 48
www.jphevin.com

L'Atelier de Joël Robuchon
5, rue Montalembert (7e)
01 42 22 56 56

133, avenue des Champs-Élysées
  (8e)
01 47 23 75 75
www.joel-robuchon.net

L'Epicuriste
41, boulevard Pasteur (15e)
01 47 34 15 50

La Coupole
102, boulevard du Montparnasse
01 43 20 14 20

La Pâtisserie des Rêves
93, rue du Bac (7e)
01 42 84 00 82

111, rue de Longchamp (16e)
01 47 04 00 24
www.lapatisseriedesreves.com

Ladurée
21, rue Bonaparte (6e)
01 44 07 64 87

16, rue Royale (8e)
01 42 60 21 79

75, avenue des
  Champs-Élysées (8e)
01 40 75 08 75
www.laduree.fr

Laura Todd
2, rue Pierre Lescot (1er)
01 42 36 15 87

47, avenue de Ségur
01 42 79 10 80
www.lauratodd.fr

Le Bistrot Paul Bert
18, rue Paul Bert (11c)
01 43 72 24 01

Le Comptoir du Relais
9, Carrefour de l'Odéon (6e)
01 44 27 07 97
www.hotel-paris-relais-saint
  -germain.com

Le Grand Vefour
17, rue du Beaujolais (1er)
01 42 96 56 27
www.grand-vefour.com

Le Moulin de la Vierge

64, rue Saint-Dominique (7e)
01 47 05 98 50

105, rue Vercingétorix (14e)
01 45 43 09 84

166, avenue de Suffren (15e)
01 47 83 45 55

6, rue de Lévis (17e)
01 43 87 42 42
www.lemoulindelavierge.com

Le Select

99, boulevard du
   Montparnasse (6e)
01 45 48 38 24

Le Verre Volé

67, rue de Lancry (10e)
01 48 03 17 34
www.leverrevole.fr

Lenôtre

10, rue Saint-Antoine (4e)
01 53 01 91 91

36, avenue de la
   Motte Piquet (7e)
01 45 55 71 25

15, boulevard de
   Courcelles (8e)
01 45 63 87 63

22, avenue de la Porte
   de Vincennes (12e)
01 43 74 54 32

91, avenue du Général
   Leclerc (14e)
01 53 90 24 50

61, rue Lecourbe (15e)
01 42 73 20 97

61, avenue de la Grande
   Armée (16e)
01 45 00 12 10

48, avenue Victor Hugo (16e)
01 45 02 21 21

44, rue d'Auteuil (16e)
01 45 24 52 52

102, avenue du
   President Kennedy (16e)
01 55 74 44 44

121, avenue de Wagram (17e)
01 47 63 70 30
www.lenotre.fr

Les Deux Abeilles

189, rue de l'Université (7e)
01 45 55 64 04

Les Deux Magots

6, place Saint-Germain-
des-Prés (6e)
01 45 48 55 25
www.lesdeuxmagots.fr

Les Petits Mitrons

26, rue Lepic (18e)
01 46 06 10 29

Lili's Brownies Café

35, rue du Dragon (6e)
01 45 49 25 03

Lola's Cookies

info@lolas-cookies.com
www.lolas-cookies.com

Merce and the Muse

1, rue Charles-François
Dupuis (3e)
06 42 39 04 31
www.merceandthemuse.com

Michel Chaudun

149, rue de l' Université (7e)
01 47 53 74 40
www.michel-chaudun.jp

Michel Cluizel

201, rue Saint-Honoré (1er)
01 42 44 11 66
www.cluizel.com

Pain de Sucre

14, rue Rambuteau (3e)
01 45 26 85 77
www.patisseriepaindesucre.com

Pierre Hermé

72, rue Bonaparte (6e)
01 43 54 47 77

4, rue Cambon (1er)
01 43 54 47 77

39, avenue de l'Opéra (2e)
01 43 54 47 77

185, rue de Vaugirard (15e)
01 47 83 89 96

58, avenue Paul Doumer (16e)
01 43 54 47 77
www.pierreherme.com

Pralus Chocolatier

35, rue Rambuteau (4e)
01 48 04 05 05
www.chocolats-pralus.com

Rose Bakery
30, rue Debelleyme (3e)
01 49 96 54 01

46, rue des Martyrs (9e)
01 42 82 12 80

10, boulevard de la Bastille (11e)
01 46 28 21 14

Sadaharu Aoki
56, boulevard de Port Royal (5e)
01 45 35 36 80

35, rue de Vaugirard (6e)
01 45 44 48 90

25, rue Pérignon (15e)
01 43 06 02 71
www.sadaharuaoki.com

Stohrer
51, rue Montorgueil (2e)
01 42 33 38 20
www.stohrer.fr

Sugar Daze
info@sugardazecupcakes.com
www.sugardazecupcakes.com/

Sweet Pea Baking
sweetpeaparis@gmail.com
www.sweetpeaparis.com

Synie's Cupcakes
23, rue de l'Abbé Grégoire (6e)
01 45 44 54 23
www.syniescupcakes.com

NEW YORK

Alice's Tea Cup

102 West Seventy-Third Street
  (Upper West Side)
212-799-3006

156 East Sixty-Fourth Street
  (Upper East Side)
212-486-9200

220 East Eighty-First Street
  (Upper East Side)
212-734-4TEA
www.alicesteacup.com

Almondine Bakery

85 Water Street (DUMBO)
718-797-5026

442 Ninth Street (Park Slope)
718-832-4607
www.almondinebakery.com

Amy's Bread

672 Ninth Avenue (Hell's Kitchen)
212-977-2670

250 Bleecker Street (West Village)
212-675-7802

75 Ninth Avenue (Chelsea Market)
212-462-4338
www.amysbread.com

Babycakes

248 Broome Street (Lower
  East Side)
212-677-5047
www.babycakesnyc.com

Baked

359 Van Brunt Street, Brooklyn
  (Red Hook)
718-222-0345
www.bakednyc.com

Baked by Melissa

7 East Fourteenth Street (Flatiron)
212-842-0220

529 Broadway (Soho)
212-842-0220

109 East Forty-Second Street
  (Grand Central)
212-842-0220

526 Seventh Avenue
  (Fashion District)
212-842-0220
www.bakedbymelissa.com

Balthazar
80 Spring Street (Soho)
212-965-1785
www.balthazarny.com

Billy's Bakery
75 Franklin Street (Tribeca)
212-647-9958

184 Ninth Avenue (Chelsea)
212-647-9956

268 Elizabeth Street (Nolita)
212-219-9956
www.billysbakerynyc.com

Birdbath
223 First Avenue (East Village)
646-722-6565

160 Prince Street (Soho)
212-612-3066

35 Third Avenue (East Village)
212-201-1902

200 Church Street (Tribeca)
212-309-7555
www.birdbathbakery.com

Bisous Ciao
101 Stanton Street
  (Lower East Side)
212-260-3463
www.bisousciao.com

Black Hound Bakery
170 Second Avenue (East Village)
212-979-9505
www.blackhoundny.com

Bond Street Chocolate
63 East Fourth Street (East Village)
212-677-5103
www.bondstchocolate.com

Bouchon Bakery
10 Columbus Circle
  (Upper West Side)
212-823-9366

1 Rockefeller Plaza
  (Upper West Side)
212-782-3890
www.bouchonbakery.com

Butter Lane
123 East Seventh Street
  (East Village)
212-677-2880
www.butterlane.com

Buttercup Bake Shop
973 Second Avenue (Midtown
  East)
212-350-4144
www.buttercupbakeshop.com

Café Deux Margot
473 Amsterdam Avenue
  (Upper West Side)
212-362-8555

Ceci-Cela
55 Spring Street (Nolita)
212-274-9179
www.cecicelanyc.com

ChikaLicious
203 East Tenth Street
  (East Village)
212-475-0929
www.chikalicious.com

City Bakery
3 West Eighteenth Street
  (Flatiron)
212-366-1414
www.thecitybakery.com

Crumbs Bake Shop
350 Amsterdam Avenue
  (Upper West Side)
212-712-9800

1675 Broadway (Midtown West)
212-399-3100

43 West Forty-Second Street
  (Midtown)
212-221-1500

2 Park Avenue (Murray Hill)
212-696-9300

37 East Eighth Street
  (Greenwich Village)
212-673-1500

1418 Lexington Avenue
  (Upper East Side)
212-360-7200

501 Madison Avenue
  (Midtown East)
212-750-0515

420 Lexington Ave.
  (Midtown East)
212-297-0500

124 University Place
  (Greenwich Village)
212-206-8011

1371 Third Avenue
  (Upper East Side)
212-794-9800

880 Third Avenue (Midtown East)
212-355-6500
www.crumbs.com

CupCake Stop
(mobile cupcake shop)
Parking locations vary.
info@cupcakestop.com
www.cupcakestop.com
@CupcakeStop

DessertTruck Works
6 Clinton Street
   (Lower East Side)
212-228-0701
www.dt-works.net

Doughnut Plant
379 Grand Street
   (Lower East Side)
212-505-3700

220 West Twenty-Third Street
   (Chelsea)
212-675-9100
www.doughnutplant.com

Duane Park Pâtisserie
179 Duane Street (Tribeca)
212-274-8447
www.duaneparkpatisserie.com

Extra Virgin
259 West Fourth Street
   (West Village)
212-691-9359
www.extravirginrestaurant.com

Financier Pâtisserie
62 Stone Street (Financial District)
212-344-5600

3-4 World Financial Center
   (Battery Park)
212-786-3220

35 Cedar Street (Financial District)
212-952-3838

983 First Avenue (Midtown East)
212-419-0100

1211 Sixth Avenue
   (Midtown West)
212-381-4418

87 East Forty-Second Street
   (Grand Central)
212-973-1010

989 Third Avenue (Midtown East)
212-486-2919

2 Astor Place (Greenwich Village)
212-228-2787

688 Sixth Avenue (Chelsea)
646-758-6238
www.financierpastries.com

François Payard
116 West Houston Street
  (Greenwich Village)
212-995-0888

FC Chocolate Bar: 1 West 58th
  Street (in Plaza Hotel)
212-986-9241
www.payard.com

Good
89 Greenwich Avenue
  (West Village)
212-691-8080
www.goodrestaurantnyc.com

Gramercy Tavern
42 East Twentieth Street
  (Flatiron)
212-477-0777
www.gramercytavern.com

Jacques Torres
66 Water Street (DUMBO)
718-875-9772

350 Hudson Street (Soho)
212-414-2462

30 Rockefeller Center
  (Midtown West)
212-664-1804

285 Amsterdam Avenue
  (Upper West Side)
212-787-3256

75 Ninth Avenue (Chelsea Market)
212-414-2462
www.mrchocolate.com

JoeDoe
45 East First Street (East Village)
212-780-0262
www.chefjoedoe.com

Kee's Chocolates
80 Thompson Street (Soho)
212-334-3284

452 Fifth Avenue (Midtown)
212-525-6099
www.keeschocolates.com

Kumquat Cupcakery
orders@kumquatcupcakery.com
www.kumquatcupcakery.com

Kyotofu
705 Ninth Avenue (Hell's Kitchen)
212-974-6012
www.kyotofu-nyc.com

La Maison du Chocolat

1018 Madison Avenue
 (Upper East Side)
212-744-7117

30 Rockefeller Center (Midtown)
212-265-9404

63 Wall Street (Financial District)
212-952-1123
www.lamaisonduchocolat.com/en/

Ladurée

864 Madison Avenue
 (Upper East Side)
646-558-3157
www.laduree.fr/en/

Lady M Cake Boutique

41 East Seventy-Eighth Street
 (Upper East Side)
212-452-2222
www.ladymconfections.com

Levain

167 West Seventy-Fourth Street
 (Upper West Side)
212-874-6080

2167 Frederick Douglass
 Boulevard (Harlem)
646-455-0952
www.levainbakery.com

Little Pie Company

424 West Forty-Third Street
 (Hell's Kitchen)
212-736-4780
www.littlepiecompany.com

Lulu Cake Boutique

112 Eighth Avenue (Chelsea)
212-242-5858
www.everythinglulu.com

Magnolia Bakery

401 Bleecker Street (West Village)
212-462-2572

200 Columbus Avenue
 (Upper West Side)
212-724-8101

1240 Avenue of the Americas
 (Theater District)
212-767-1123

107 East Forty-Second Street
 (Grand Central)
212-682-3588
www.magnoliabakery.com

Make My Cake

2380 Adam Clayton Powell
 Boulevard (Harlem)
212-234-2344

121 St. Nicholas Avenue
  (Harlem)
212-932-0833
www.makemycake.com

Momofuku Milk Bar
15 West Fifty-Sixth Street
  (Midtown West)
212-757-5878

251 East Thirteenth Street
  (East Village)
212-254-3500

382 Metropolitan Avenue,
  Brooklyn (Williamsburg)
www.momofuku.com

Out of the Kitchen
420 Hudson Street (West Village)
212-242-0399
www.outofthekitchenonline.com

Pastis
9 Ninth Avenue
  (Meatpacking District)
212-929-4844
www.pastisny.com

Pâtisserie Claude
187 West Fourth Street
  (West Village)
212-255-5911

Prune
54 East First Street (East Village)
212-677-6221
www.prunerestaurant.com

Roni-Sue's Chocolates
120 Essex Street (Lower East Side)
212-260-0421
www.roni-sue.com

Ruby et Violette
457 West Fiftieth Street
  (Hell's Kitchen)
212-582-6720
www.rubyetviolette.com

Spot Dessert Bar
13 St. Mark's Place (East Village)
212-677-5670
www.spotdessertbar.com

Sugar Sweet Sunshine
126 Rivington Street
  (Lower East Side)
212-995-1960
www.sugarsweetsunshine.com

Sweet and Vicious
5 Spring Street (Nolita)
212-334-7915
www.sweetandviciousnyc.com

Sweet Revenge
62 Carmine Street (West Village)
212-242-2240
www.sweetrevengenyc.com

Teuscher
620 Fifth Avenue
   (Rockefeller Plaza)
212-246-4416
www.teuscherfifthavenue.com

25 East Sixty-First Street
   (Upper East Side)
212-751-8482
www.teuschermadison.com
www.teuscher-newyork.com

Thé Adoré
17 East Thirteenth Street
   (Greenwich Village)
212-243-8742

Tu-Lu's Gluten-Free Bakery
338 East Eleventh Street
   (East Village)
212-777-2227
www.tu-lusbakery.com

Two Little Red Hens
1652 Second Avenue
   (Upper East Side)
212-452-0476
www.twolittleredhens.com

Vosges Haut-Chocolat
1100 Madison Avenue
   (Upper East Side)
212-717-2929

132 Spring Street (Soho)
212-625-2929
www.vosgeschocolate.com

ABOUT THE AUTHOR

Photo by Lindsey Tramuta.

Amy Thomas is a New York–based writer who, for two lucky years, got to call Paris home. In addition to working as a copywriter in advertising, she writes about food, travel, design, and fashion for various publications such as the *New York Times, National Geographic Traveler, Town & Country,* and *Every Day with Rachel Ray.* She is slightly obsessed with sweets.

PARIS MAP KEY

 A l'Etoile d'Or   30, rue Fontaine

 Angelina   226, rue de Rivoli

 Au 35   35, rue Jacob

 Blé Sucré   7, rue Antoine Vollon

 Cupcakes & Co   25, rue de la Forgé Royale

 Du Pain et Des Idées   34, rue Yves Toudic

 Eric Kayser   16, rue des Petits-Carreaux

 Jean-Paul Hévin   231, rue Saint-Honoré

 La Coupole   102, boulevard du Montparnasse

 Ladurée   75, avenue Champs-Élysées

 Les Deux Abeilles   189, rue de l'Université

 Pierre Hermé   72, rue Bonaparte

 Rose Bakery   46, rue des Martyrs

Stohrer   51, rue Montorgueil

NYC MAP KEY

 Billy's Bakery   184 Ninth Avenue

 Buttercup Bake Shop   973 Second Avenue

 City Bakery   3 West Eighteenth Street

 Jacques Torres   62 Water Street

 Joe Doe   45 East First Street

 Kee's Chocolates   80 Thompson Street

 Lady M   41 East Seventy-Eighth Street

 Levain Bakery   167 West Seventy-Fourth Street

 Magnolia Bakery   401 Bleecker Street

 Make My Cake   121 St. Nicholas Avenue (Harlem)

 Momofuku Milk Bar   251 East Thirteenth Street

 Patisserie Claude   187 West Fourth Street

 Spot Dessert Bar   13 St. Mark's Place

 Thé Adoré   17 East Thirteenth Street